The Auth

Maralene and Miles Wesner are multi-talented teachers and prolific writers. They have published more than 150 Audio-Visual Education aids, and pioneered new reading methods with their Phonics in a Nutshell (1965).

They have written articles, and mission studies for Southern Baptist periodicals. They were in the original group of writers to develop WMU's Big "A" Club material.

They've published several books with Broadman Press: *A Fresh Look at the Gospel* (1983); *You Are What You Choose* (1984); and *How To Be a Saint When You Feel Like a Sinner* (1986) and self-published 30 books by Diversity Press.

They are noted for their no-nonsense style, their clear illustrations, and their willingness to face controversial issues. From the dual perspectives of both academic and religious professions, they seek to be a bridge between the spiritual and the intellectual worlds.

They hold Masters Degrees (MEd) from Oklahoma University plus work toward a Doctorate. Miles also attended Southwestern Baptist Theological Seminary, and served as a high school counselor. He has been the bi-vocational pastor of a small rural church for more than 50 years.

Both Maralene and Miles taught in public school and collages and served as educational consultants. Maralene taught Psychology and Speech for Southeastern Oklahoma State University for 32 years. She was chosen Oklahoma Teacher of the Year in 1975.

They have planned, led tours, and done research in all of the 50 states, Canada, Mexico, Europe, Egypt, Japan, and the Holy Land. In 1985, they were among a small group of Americans who were invited by Dr. Joseph P. Kennedy of the US/China Education Foundation and Bishop Ting, leader of the Three Self Movement, to participate in the First Symposium on the Church in Nanjing, China.

Now, they use their lifetime of varied experiences to write insightful sermons, essays, and books.

Titles by Maralene & Miles Wesner
published by Nurturing Faith

Sermons for Special Days

Life More Abundant

LIFE MORE
Abundant

Maralene & Miles Wesner

© 2021
Published in the United States by Nurturing Faith, Macon, GA.
Nurturing Faith is a book imprint of Good Faith Media (goodfaithmedia.org).
Library of Congress Cataloging-in-Publication Data is available.

ISBN: 978-1-63528-151-4

Cover image by David Cassady.

Contents

Preface

This book presents a psychological explanation of the gospel. It deals with the nine basic human needs that salvation fills.

Believing that we have acceptance, love, and value gives us peace and contentment: "We have peace with God through our Lord Jesus Christ" (Rom 5:1).

Believing that we have security, forgiveness, and guidance gives us assurance and confidence: "All things can be done for the one who believes" (Mark 9:23).

Believing that we have support, purpose, and hope gives us meaning and significance: "We have this hope, a sure and steadfast anchor for the soul" (Heb 6:19).

People today want more than creeds and platitudes. Discovering that there are logical reasons for the positive changes that take place when we become a Christian helps us understand how and why a conversion experience makes such a real difference in our lives.

Part 1:
The Need for Abundant Life

Jesus said, "I came that they may have life, and have it abundantly" (John 10:10).

Many people live lives of "quiet desperation." Shakespeare described such a pitiful existence in his tragedy *Macbeth*: "Life's but a walking shadow, a poor player that struts and frets his hour upon the stage and then is heard no more. It is a tale told by an idiot, full of sound and fury—signifying nothing."

Jesus, however, offers something much better. He offers the kind of life that fulfills not only our *eternal* needs, but our earthly needs. Furthermore, if our needs were truly filled, destructive addictions like alcoholism, drugs, gambling, promiscuity, and compulsive shopping would disappear. That's because people who succumb to these vices are really attempting to satisfy legitimate human cravings. They are trying to eliminate their feelings of emptiness, abolish their misery, and fill their needs.

Unfortunately, these things don't satisfy. They only create more problems. The psalmist said, "He satisfies the thirsty, and the hungry he fills with good things" (Ps 107:9). Paul, too, gives us a wonderful promise: "God will fully satisfy every need of yours according to his riches in glory in Christ Jesus" (Phil 4:19).

So what are these deep, unfulfilled needs that make us miserable and cause us to destroy our lives? More importantly, how does the gospel of Jesus fill these needs and give us abundant life? In this book we'll examine these nine basic needs that must be filled in order to have the abundant life Jesus gives.

1. *Acceptance*: As human beings we tend to judge and rebuff each other. Because of this most of us have been so slighted and alienated over the years that we feel rejected. But Jesus offers total acceptance: "Everything that the Father gives me will come to me, and anyone who comes to me I will never drive away" (John 6:37).

2. *Love*: As human beings we tend to criticize and revile each other. Because of this most of us have been so hurt and despised over the years that we feel unloved. But Jesus offers unconditional *love*: "As the Father has loved me, so I have loved you; … No one has greater love than this, to lay down one's life for one's friends" (John 15:9, 13).

3. *Value*: As human beings we tend to degrade and dishonor each other. Because of this most of us have been so disrespected and humiliated over the years that we feel worthless. But Jesus emphasizes our *value*: "Do not be afraid; you are of more value than many sparrows" (Matt 10:31).

4. *Security*: As human beings we tend to intimidate and threaten each other. Because of this most of us have been so put down and bullied over the years that we feel insecure. But Jesus offers absolute *security*: "Peace I leave with you; my peace I give to you…. Do not let your hearts be troubled, and do not let them be afraid" (John 14:27).

5. *Forgiveness*: As human beings we tend to blame and accuse each other. Because of this most of us have been so shamed and condemned over the years that we feel guilty. But Jesus offers complete *forgiveness*: "Very truly, I tell you, anyone who hears my word and believes him who sent me has eternal life, and does not come under judgment" (John 5:24).

6. *Guidance*: As human beings we tend to have different opinions and get different advice. Because of this most of us have made so many wrong decisions over the years that we feel confused. But Jesus offers *guidance*: "When the Spirit of truth comes, he will guide you into all the truth" (John 16:13).

7. *Support*: As human beings we tend to withdraw and abandon each other in a crisis. Because of this most of us have been so let down and disappointed over the years that we feel helpless. But Jesus offers his presence and full *support*: "Remember, I am with you always, to the end of the age" (Matt 28:20).

8. *Purpose*: As human beings we tend to be apathetic and undisciplined. Because of this most us have become so aimless and unfocused over the years that we feel frustrated. But Jesus gives us *purpose*: "Go therefore and make disciples of all nations…teaching them to obey everything that I have commanded you" (Matt 28:19–20).

9. *Hope*: As human beings we tend to experience depression and misery. Because of this most of us become so discouraged and pessimistic over the years that we feel despair. But Jesus gives us *hope* and joy: "I have said these things to so that my joy may be in you, and that your joy may be complete" (John 15:11).

It's obvious that every individual has basic needs: acceptance, love, value, security, forgiveness, guidance, support, purpose, and hope. If any of these needs are unmet, we feel empty and incomplete. That why Jesus offers salvation. Over and over during his ministry on earth, when the Lord met hurting people, he would declare, "You are made whole." He meant, "All of your needs are filled, and you lack nothing."

Once, an old minister responded to an atheist by saying, "Sir, if I discovered that there is no God and my faith was an illusion, I wouldn't change a thing. My Christian life has given me so many benefits that I don't regret my decision to embrace it.'"

Then he listed these nine basic benefits:

1. "I was *accepted* by my church family."
2. "I felt *loved* by God and my fellow Christians."
3. "My work in the church gave me a feeling of *value*."
4. "I experienced peace and *security* instead of anxiety and insecurity."
5. "I was *forgiven*, and my guilt was abolished."
6. "I was strengthened and *guided* in times of uncertainty."
7. "I had a loyal *support* group during sorrow and tragedy."
8. "My faith gave meaning and *purpose* to my life."
9. "I had *hope* instead of despair."

If something consistently produces such positive results, then it's *real*. When we realize these benefits, then we can experience the abundant life Jesus promised.

According to legend, the little boy who gave Jesus his loaves and fishes saw Jesus's miracle and said, "Wow! If he can do that with my lunch, what could he do with my whole life?" Each of us might ask the same thing: What if I gave him my whole life? What if I gave him my time? Would my day look different? Would he enable me to accomplish more of his work? What if I gave him my talents? Would I discover some hidden special abilities? Would he develop them more fully? Would he allow me to influence every life I encounter? What if I gave him my treasure? Would I be able to invest in things that will last throughout eternity? What if I didn't stop at time, talents, and treasure? What if I gave him my hopes and my dreams?"

That's the way to realize abundant life! Jesus said, "For those who want to save their life will lose it, and those who lose their life for my sake, and for the sake of the gospel, will save it" (Mark 8:35b).

God can ease every pain, soothe every fear, and fill every need. That's what Jesus offered when he said, "I came that they may have life, and have it abundantly" (John 10:10).

Life is precious. If a medicine were produced today that guaranteed physical life, it would be in great demand. Suppose there was such a capsule. If a person was involved in a fatal accident, the medic could slip that capsule in the victim's mouth, and immediately life would return. If a patient died on an operating table, the doctor could administer the medicine, and all would be well.

If there was a pill that would ensure only one day of additional life, people would panic to get it. Just suppose a pill was produced that would give everlasting life. People would beg, borrow, or steal to get enough money to purchase it. No effort would be spared in order to mass-produce the product. Long lines would form in front of all the businesses that sold it. The demand would be overwhelming.

The doctor discovering it would be praised. His fame would make his name a household word. His popularity would be unexcelled.

Well, Jesus did just that! And he offers not only life, but abundant life!

Acceptance

One of our most basic human needs is the need for acceptance. A few years ago, a man walked into a gym, turned off the lights, and fired his gun more than thirty times. He killed several women in an aerobics class and then turned the gun on himself. The note he left behind read, "3,000 women have rejected me."

Not everyone who feels rejected becomes a mass murderer, but the pain of rejection is a prevalent pain and one of the hardest to bear. Abandoned children, handicapped individuals, those of minority races, and the elderly in nursing homes may feel it most acutely, but all of us feel it at times.

Negative Effects of Rejection

The negative effects of rejection are numerous. In order to develop successfully, a child must feel he belongs in his family; he must feel wanted. People are often reluctant to ask for dates or apply for jobs or even come to church because they are afraid of rejection. Rejection says, "You are not okay! You are not adequate! You are inferior!" And that hurts.

Furthermore, these negative effects are far reaching. People who feel rejected degrade themselves and then project that degradation onto others. Such individuals have negative outlooks and critical spirits. Consider the story of woman lived in an apartment and could look across the alley into the neighboring apartment. After several months, the woman began to notice that the neighbor's windows were very dirty. Everything was a blur through the smudged glass. The woman wondered why the lazy neighbors would not wash their windows. One morning, the woman cleaned her own windows, then sat down to rest. Looking out across the alley, she was surprised that she could see clearly into the neighboring apartment. That's when it dawned on Her that she had been criticizing *the neighbor's* dirty windows when all the time the dirty window was *her own!*

How often do we criticize others through our own "dirty windows" of ignorance and inferiority? Such destructive sins are often the result of our feelings of rejection. Jesus said, "Why do you see the speck in your neighbor's eye, but do not notice the log in your own eye?" (Matt 7:3).

Rejection also leads to shame and humiliation. These dangerous emotions make us defensive and hostile. Unfortunately, traditional religion has often tended to increase the problem by diminishing life instead of enriching it. Some Christian groups seem to emphasize doctrines that condemn people. The story goes that a man with some personal issues was excommunicated and forbidden to enter a church. He took his woes to God. "Lord," he said, "they won't let me in because I'm a sinner."

"What are you complaining about?" God replied. "They won't let me in either!"

Often, sinners hobble into our churches for Sunday morning worship services on crutches of addictions and sinful habits, but their mere presence represents a feeble attempt to establish contact with God. We must not discourage that hope. A minister said, "A few years ago I heard a song on the radio that I liked. The lyrics were talking about a place where 'everybody knows your name, and they're always glad you came.' Then someone told me it was the theme song for a TV show about a bar. I still wish they'd been singing it about the church." Well, it should be the motto of every congregation because any church that will not accept sinful men and women repudiates the gospel of grace.

God knows that faith is weak, knowledge is limited, and people are imperfect. If Christians remain self-righteously aloof from those who fail and those who fall, they are not following Jesus's example. He said, "I have come to call not the righteous but sinners" (Matt 9:13).

Rejection is unproductive. It never converts anyone! Jesus came to give us abundant life, and no one can enjoy an abundant life without acceptance.

Positive Effects of Acceptance

Acceptance is an important theme of the gospel because there are many positive effects of acceptance. In fact, acceptance is essential for an abundant life. Jesus never rejects anyone. He said, "Anyone who comes to me I will never drive away" (John 6:37).

Then the Lord practiced what he promised by accepting all who came to him. When children were being turned away, Jesus said, "'Let the little children come to me, and do not stop them; for it is to such as these that the kingdom of heaven belongs" (Matt 19:14).

Then, when a very sinful woman ministered to him, he accepted her. Scripture says,

> And a woman in the city, who was a sinner, having learned
> that he was eating in the Pharisee's house, brought an

alabaster jar of ointment. She stood behind him at his feet, weeping, and began to bathe his feet with her tears and to dry them with her hair. Then she continued kissing his feet and anointing them with the ointment. Now when the Pharisee who had invited him saw it, he said to himself, "If this man were a prophet, he would have known who and what kind of woman this is who is touching him—that she is a sinner." Jesus spoke up and said to him, "Simon, I have something to say to you." "Teacher," he replied, "speak." "A certain creditor had two debtors; one owed five hundred denarii, and the other fifty. When they could not pay, he canceled the debts for both of them. Now which of them will love him more?" Simon answered, "I suppose the one for whom he canceled the greater debt." And Jesus said to him, "You have judged rightly." Then turning toward the woman, he said to Simon, "Do you see this woman? I entered your house; you gave me no water for my feet, but she has bathed my feet with her tears and dried them with her hair. You gave me no kiss, but from the time I came in she has not stopped kissing my feet. You did not anoint my head with oil, but she has anointed my feet with ointment. Therefore, I tell you, her sins, which were many, have been forgiven; hence she has shown great love. But the one to whom little is forgiven, loves little." (Luke 7:37–47)

At other times sinners and undesirables came to Jesus. Matthew said, "And as he sat at dinner in the house, many tax collectors and sinners came and were sitting with him and his disciples. When the Pharisees saw this, they said to his disciples, 'Why does your teacher eat with tax collectors and sinners?' But when he heard this, he said, 'Those who are well have no need of a physician, but those who are sick'" (Matt 9:10–12)[1].

In first-century Judaism the class system was rigorously enforced. Orthodox individuals were legally forbidden to associate with those who were outside the Law. Table fellowship with beggars, prostitutes, and tax collectors was a religious and social taboo. These tax collectors were considered traitors because they took money for Rome from their own people and received a kickback from the take. Furthermore, sharing a meal was a special dramatic sign of equality and acceptance. That's why Zacchaeus was so moved when Jesus called him down from the sycamore tree, and that's why Jesus's practice of eating with such people caused so many hostile comments throughout his ministry.

Repeatedly, we see Jesus accepting traitors, lepers, foreigners, and other outcasts. This is important because people who feel accepted respect themselves and thus are able to extend that same respect to others. They have positive outlooks and helpful spirits.

Acceptance helps us experience an abundant life!

How to Realize Acceptance

If all of us have such a desperate need for acceptance, how can we realize it in our daily lives? We are fortunate as Christians because the scriptures give us many promises concerning acceptance. The psalmist said, "Then I acknowledged my sin to you, and I did not hide my iniquity. I said, 'I will confess my transgressions to the LORD,' and you forgave the guilt of my sin" (Ps 32:5).

Jesus said, "I give them eternal life, and they will never perish. No one will snatch them out of my hand" (John 10:28).

Paul said, "While we were still sinners Christ died for us" (Rom 5:8).

John said, "In this is love, not that we loved God but that he loved us" (1 John 4:10).

In his wonderful parable, Jesus told how the prodigal son came to his father and was immediately accepted and restored without any condemnation or rehabilitation. Instead, there was a celebration (see Luke 15:22–24).

When we come to God through Christ, we are born into God's family. At that moment we are accepted totally, and we are accepted permanently. Like the prodigal son, there is no condemnation or rehabilitation. Instead, there is a celebration. Jesus said, "'I tell you, there will be more joy in heaven over one sinner who repents than over ninety-nine righteous persons who need no repentance'" (Luke 15:7). This conversion changes our lives. When we are able to feel God's acceptance, our relief and gratitude for this great gift makes us want to please our heavenly Father. It makes us try harder to be obedient and faithful. It makes us eager to witness and serve in his kingdom.

Let's consider a spiritual analogy: You've just been born and are taking your first breath. The doctor and nurse are smiling, but your parents are strangely preoccupied. They confer quietly with each other, ignoring your cries. Finally, the father turns to the physician and says, "Doctor, would you mind holding that baby up once more so we can better decide?"

"Decide what?" the doctor asks.

"We just want to be sure he's right for us," your father replies. "We saw another child in the nursery that seems to have a little more promise. This baby's eyes are the wrong color, and its nose is too big. You see, we really have our hearts set on that cute little blond baby. My wife and I have discussed this, and we'd like to work out an exchange."

Obviously, this scenario is totally absurd. When you were born, your parents accepted you into their hearts and into their family without hesitations or qualifications. This acceptance was not based on your looks. It was not based on your performance. It was not even based on your behavior. They accepted you simply because you were their child.

That's how God accepts us! As a Christian you are accepted just as you are, with all your faults and shortcomings, with all your failures and problems. You are accepted, and you will never be rejected.

A doctor said, "Eighty percent of my patients could be cured of the physical ills that plague them if only they had one non-judgmental, understanding person who would listen to them with respect, care for them as an individual, and accept them just as they are." God does that for us. How can we realize this wonderful gift from God? How can we feel accepted and then pass on that gift to others? To do this we must believe that Jesus offers us not only life, but abundant life! And abundant life includes acceptance.

Note
[1] Brennan Manning, *The Ragamuffin Gospel* (Colorado Springs: WaterBrook Multnomah) 57

Love

One of our most basic human needs is the need for love. A television emcee was once asked, "What are you most afraid of?" His reply was, "I have to admit that the thing I am most afraid of is not being loved."

We've laughed at a comedian, but we can identify with his first joke. He said that as a little boy, in a game of hide and seek, he hid, but nobody came to seek him. To feel that nobody is seeking you, that nobody wants you, is one of the hardest things to bear.

Love is as important as food and drink. Human babies cannot develop properly without it. People from dysfunctional families and abusive situations suffer the most, but all of us have love needs.

Negative Effects of Lack of Love

The negative effects of the lack of love are very harmful. Children need to be touched and cuddled. Such warm contact tells us there is someone out there we can trust and depend on. Our hope for getting our needs met depends on this. If we can feel the presence of an emotionally available person, we can begin our life with a sense of trust. We can believe that the world is friendly and that our needs will be filled. If a nurturing person is not there for us, we begin to mistrust the world. We have to create an illusion of connectedness in order to go on. This leads to addictions and destructive relationships.

Every person yearns for love. Babies die from lack of love. Unfortunately, most of us hide our desire for love, even from ourselves. We say, "I don't need anybody," or we try to earn love by becoming a people-pleaser. We may even seek attention as a substitute for love by misbehaving, breaking the law, or becoming promiscuous.

People who are deprived of love cannot extend love. They are empty. They feel cheated. It's unfortunate that critical and unpleasant individuals are actually revealing their desperate craving for love. A man named Van came from a hostile, dysfunctional family. As an adult he "got religion," but it was a loveless, legalistic religion. Almost immediately Van began to condemn his siblings for their rebelliousness toward God. He preached and "Bible-bullied" and shamed them. They didn't measure up to his expectations. Just as his father had berated him, Van began to berate those around him.

When Van made an acquaintance, he would begin to notice their short-comings. He would demean them for their lack of commitment. His father's abuse came from alcohol. Van's abuse came from religion. As he became even more fanatical, he would stay up all night at a mission for street people and then not show up for work the next day. His employers became tired of this and gave him an ultimatum. If his absenteeism continued, he would be fired.

Van responded indignantly and continued to preach the "godly" lifestyle to his fellow workers and to show up late, if at all. Finally, his employers discharged him. Van deluded himself into believing that all these people were atheists who were persecuting him for his faith.

You see, even religion without love can be evil. Paul said, "If I have prophetic powers, and understand all mysteries and all knowledge, and if I have all faith, so as to remove mountains, but do not have love, I am nothing" (1 Cor 13:2).

People without love are destructive. Empathy, compassion, and fellow-ship are absolutely essential. A scene in the play *Godspell* shows Jesus taking a bucket of water, a rag, and a mirror to each disciple. One by one, he washes away their painted clown faces. Then he holds up the mirror so they can see themselves as they really are. The point is obvious: We don't have to wear false faces. We don't have to hide our weaknesses and faults. We don't have to pretend to be something we're not. God loves us just as we are. We call that "amazing grace."

Jesus came to give us abundant life, and no one can enjoy abundant life without love.

Positive Effects of Feeling Loved

Love is an important theme of the gospel because there are many positive effects of love. In fact, love is essential for *abundant life*. Love turns sinners into saints. Jesus personified love. He said, "'As the Father has loved me, so I have loved you; abide in my love. This is my commandment, that you love one another as I have loved you'" (John 15:9, 12).

Jesus brought love to a new level. Of course he loved his followers. That's not surprising. The scriptures say, "Having loved his own who were in the world, he loved them to the end" (John 13:1).

Then he loved some special friends: "Jesus loved Martha and her sister and Lazarus" (John 11:5).

He loved the "rich young ruler" even as he walked away. Mark says, "Jesus, looking at the him, loved him and said, 'You lack one thing: go, sell what you own, and give the money to the poor…then come, follow me.' When he heard this, he was shocked and went away grieving, for he had many possessions" (see Mark 10:21–22).

The surprising difference about Jesus is that he also loved his enemies: "'You have heard that it was said, "You shall love your neighbor and hate your enemy." But I say to you, love your enemies" (Matt 5:43–44).

He explained this unusual command, saying, "'If you love those who love you, what credit is that to you? For even sinners love those who love them. If you do good to those who do good to you, what credit is that to you? For even sinners do the same. If you lend to those from whom you hope to receive, what credit is that to you? Even sinners lend to sinners, to receive as much again. But love your enemies, do good, and lend, expecting nothing in return. Your reward will be great, and you will be children of the Most High; for he is kind to the ungrateful and the wicked'" (see Luke 6:32–35).

This kind of love is more than an emotion. It is not just affection. Instead, it extends respect and justice to all. Love changes our lives and enables us to change other lives. Those who feel loved are affectionate and caring. They are able to extend goodwill and charity to those around them.

A woman was married to a tyrant of a husband. He didn't like the way she cooked. He didn't like the way she ran the home. He didn't like the way she dressed. He constantly criticized her for everything.

Finally, he handed her a list of twenty-five rules she was supposed to follow. Oh, how she hated him! You can imagine the frustration of constantly checking that list to see if she was pleasing him and staying out of trouble. She usually failed miserably, and each time she got a tongue-lashing.

Then, unexpectedly, her abusive husband died. Later, she fell in love with and married a wonderful, loving husband. Her life was pleasant, and she worked hard to please him.

One day, she ran across that old list. Suddenly, she began to laugh! As she checked the items, she realized she was now doing all of these things—and many more—for her new husband. Furthermore, she did them with great joy because she loved him.

This demonstrates a great spiritual truth concerning our relationship with God. Love makes all the difference. We do not have to change and grow and be good in order for God to love us. Rather, God loves us, and that enables us to change and grow and be good.

Love helps us experience an abundant life!

How to Realize Love

If all of us have such a desperate need for love, then how can we realize it in our daily lives? We are fortunate as Christians because the scriptures give us many promises concerning love. The psalmist said, "How precious is your steadfast love" (Ps 36:7).

Jesus said, "For God so loved the world that he gave his only Son, so that everyone who believes in him may not parish but may have eternal life" (John 3:16).

Paul said, "Who will separate us from the love of Christ?" (Rom 8:35).

Later, he said, "For I am convinced that neither…height, nor depth, nor anything else in all creation, will be able to separate us from the love of God in Christ Jesus our Lord" (Rom 8:38–39).

John said, "Beloved, since God loved us so much, we also ought to love one another" (1 John 4:11).

When we come to God through Christ, we are assured of the love of our heavenly Father and of our Christian brothers and sisters. Such love frees us to serve others. Christian love is a special, unconditional love.

If love is conditional love. It says, "I love you *if* you agree with me, *if* you help me, *if* you do what I say, *if* you measure up to my standards."

Because love is easy love. It says, "I love you *because* you are like me, *because* you helped me, *because* you're agreeable, *because* you make me look good."

Anyway love is Christlike love. It says, "I love you *anyway*, even if you are different; *anyway*, even if you don't agree with me; *anyway*, even if you refuse to help me; *anyway*, even if you don't understand me and my lifestyle. Yes, I love you anyway because that's how God loves me!"

In fact, one of the greatest rewards of salvation is the awareness of God's unconditional, undying love.

A father said, "Yesterday, my daughter Gretchen and I were out in the garden. Gretchen picked a daisy and said, 'Daddy, this flower is for God.' As she pulled the first petal, she said, 'He loves me.' Then she pulled the next and said, 'He loves me.' Until she had but one petal left, smiling brightly, she finished the rhyme, 'He loves me.'"

That is the gospel. There are no "he loves me not" petals in Christ's gospel.

Once, a man traveled a long way to visit a relative with Alzheimer's disease, but there was no response to his greeting. He couldn't establish communication or evoke a memory. Finally, just before he left, sad and disappointed, he asked one more time, "Do you know who I am, dear?" At that moment a smile broke through and a soft voice whispered, "Yes, you're somebody who loves me."

The man explained, "They may have been the only words she spoke during my visit, but they said it all!" What else do we need to know about one another and about God? When we're not sure of anything else, we can still say to our heavenly Father with joyful certainty, "I know one thing: You are somebody who loves me!"

How can we realize this wonderful gift from God? How can we feel loved and then pass on that gift to others? To do this we must believe Jesus offers us not only life, but abundant life. And abundant life includes love.

Value

One of our most basic human needs is the need for value. A certain bright-eyed little third-grader loved his teacher, but he failed all his tests and lost all his homework. One day, the exasperated teacher looked at him and said, "Young man, you are very smart, and you could be one of my best students." Then, before she could finish scolding him, he looked up at her with large, serious eyes and said, "I didn't know that!"

From then on, things were different. This child *did* become one of her best students. You see, when he realized his value, it changed his life.

Negative Effects of Feeling Worthless

The negative effects of worthlessness are deadly. Being deprived of attention and approval can literally kill a child in the earliest stages of life. As we grow older, our need for physical strokes is extended into the need for emotional strokes. This means being noticed, being respected, being valued, and being recognized for our achievements.

Children will demand attention, but adults often deny this need. They seem to be embarrassed by compliments and appreciation. But they still need them.

Strokes are to the psyche what food is to the body. When we can't get this need filled in a legitimate manner, we'll do whatever we have to do to get it. Children who do not get strokes in a healthy way will get them in unhealthy ways. Being singled out as bad, causing trouble, or becoming the family failure are all negative ways of getting recognition.

Our "value mark" gets set at an early age and affects us the rest of our lives. People who feel worthless will live down to that evaluation. They will allow and even seek out abuse. They will actually sabotage their own success and happiness because they don't feel they deserve it.

Some individuals' need for approval can be so great that they become workaholics or people-pleasers. Furthermore, they filter life situations through a negative lens. They discount what's right and look for what's wrong. Nothing is ever good enough! According to legend, a farmer once took his new hunting dog out for a "test run." Presently, he shot a duck. The dog walked out on the water, retrieved the duck, and brought it in. The farmer rubbed his eyes and tried again with the same result.

Bewildered and completely flabbergasted, he invited an unusually pessimistic and critical neighbor to go with him the following day. True to form, when either man hit a bird, the dog would *walk out on the water* and retrieve it. The neighbor said nothing. The farmer said nothing. Finally, unable to hold it in a moment longer, the owner of the dog blurted out, "Say, fellow, did you notice anything unusual about my dog?"

The neighbor rubbed his chin reflectively. "Yeah," he said at last. "Yeah, come to think of it, I did. That dog *can't swim*, can he?"

Such negative individuals reveal their own feelings of inferiority. Our self-image reflects the value we put on ourselves. A poor self-image, based on a sense of inferiority, will affect our attitudes toward ourselves, our family, our friends, and God. It can make us do unproductive things that compound our problems. We may resist authority, both earthly and divine; we may use wrong methods to gain acceptance; we may become preoccupied with the way we look; we may daydream about being someone else.

Few issues in the Christian faith are more misunderstood than this idea about self-esteem and self-worth. Scripture teaches us on one hand that we must value ourselves. Jesus said, "'Love your neighbor as yourself'" (Matt 22:39). At the same time, Scripture condemns pride: "If those who are nothing think they are something, they deceive themselves" (Gal 6:3).

The proper balance is a self-concept that recognizes that God gave us our value and we can't be worthless when Christ is in our life. Jesus came to give us abundant life, and no one can enjoy an abundant life without a sense of self-value!

Positive Effects of Feeling Valued

Value is an important theme of the gospel because there are many positive effects of feeling valuable. In fact, value is essential for abundant life. Jesus emphasized the value of each unique individual: "Are not two sparrows sold for a penny? Yet not one of them will fall to the ground apart from your Father. And even the hairs of your head are all counted. So do not be afraid; you are of more value than many sparrows" (Matt 10:29–31).

Jesus practiced this philosophy of goodwill toward others. When Mary chose an unusual activity for a woman of that day, he supported her. Martha had complained that Mary was discussing theology with Jesus instead of helping her in the kitchen, but he answered, "There is need of only one thing.

Mary has chosen the better part, which will not be taken away from her" (Luke 10:42).

Jesus saw and encouraged the worth of a sinful woman who anointed his feet with perfume. When the Pharisee who asked Jesus to come to his house saw this, he thought to himself, "'If this man were a prophet, he would have known who and what kind of woman this is who is touching him—that she is a sinner.'... [Jesus] said to Simon, 'Do you see this woman? I entered your house; you gave me no water for my feet, but she has bathed my feet with her tears and dried them with her hair.... You did not anoint my head with oil, but she has anointed my feet with ointment. Therefore, I tell you, her sins, which were many, have been forgiven'" (see Luke 7:37–39, 44–47).

He also said, "'Wherever this good news is proclaimed in the whole world, what she has done will be told in remembrance of her" (Matt 26:13).

Jesus even gave value to a hated traitor and thief named Zacchaeus. Scripture says, "A man was there named Zacchaeus; he was a chief tax collector and was rich.... All who saw [Jesus go to his house] began to grumble, 'He has gone to be the guest of one who is a sinner!'... Jesus said to him, 'Today salvation has come to this house, because he too is a son of Abraham'" (see Luke 19:2, 7, 9).

God deals with individuals. It is said that Julia Ward Howe wrote a senator on behalf of a man who was in trouble. The senator replied that he was so busy with the affairs of the nation that he could not take time for individuals. Her answer was, "Fortunately, God hasn't reached this point." She was right. In the parable Jesus did not speak of a lost flock, but of one lost sheep.

Jesus knew that we live either up or down to the labels we are given, so he gave Peter a new name to live up to: "You are Peter, and on this rock I will build my church, and the gates of Hades will not prevail against it. I will give you the keys of the kingdom of heaven, and whatever you bind on earth will be bound in heaven, and whatever you loose on earth will be loosed in heaven" (see Matt 16:18–19).

This transfer of power shows that God values us as representatives. When a certain wealthy humanitarian was questioned about the reasons for his great success, he explained, "As a child I almost drowned, and a man rescued me. When I thanked him, he replied, 'You're welcome, son. You were worth saving.' That statement determined my 'philosophy of life.' I knew I had to live up to that!"

People who have value see worth in themselves and others. They can succeed because they feel they deserve success. They don't let people abuse them, and they don't abuse others. They tend to see the positive and ignore the negative.

Value helps us experience an abundant life!

How to Realize Value

If all of us have such a desperate need for value, then how can we realize it in our daily lives? We're fortunate as Christians because the scriptures give many promises concerning our value. Scripture says, "God created humankind in his image, in the image of God he created them; male and female he created them" (Gen 1:27).

Isaiah illustrates God's attitude toward us by using a dramatic analogy: "Can a woman forget her nursing child…? Even these may forget, yet I will not forget you!" (Isa 49:15).

The psalmist said, "What are human beings that you are mindful of them, mortals that you care for them? Yet you have made them a little lower than God, and crowned them with glory and honor. You have given them dominion over the works of your hands; you have put all things under their feet" (Ps 8:4–6). Later, he said, "I praise you, for I am fearfully and wonderfully made" (Ps 139:14).

John said, "In this is love, not that we loved God but that he loved us" (1 John 4:10).

In God's eyes there is no such thing as an anonymous person. Jesus died to make "somebodies" out of "nobodies"! When we realize our value, then we will value others. The great poet John Donne wrote in "Meditation 17" (1623):

> No man is an island—entire of itself.
> Every man is a piece of the continent;
> A part of the main.
> Any man's death diminishes me
> Because I am involved in mankind.
> Therefore, never send to know for whom the bell tolls.
> It tolls for thee.

One man said, "As a child I learned to grieve at funerals, even if I didn't know who had died. I was taught that when any man or woman dies, something very valuable had passed. I'd sit there and just cry along with the family. You don't just let a person die as though nothing has happened. You must understand that a great loss has been suffered."

Every individual has infinite value.

There is a story about a young boy in Austria giving his first violin recital. He had studied for years under one of the great masters. The youth had tremendous talent, and he had learned his lessons well. Before an audience of hundreds, he performed with confidence and skill. Following each piece, the crowd clapped and cheered. Yet the boy didn't seem to notice their expressions of approval.

At the conclusion of the recital, the entire audience rose to give the young prodigy a standing ovation. They shouted "Bravo!" and "Encore!" and other words of praise. Strangely, the young musician seemed almost distracted as he stood looking up into the balcony. Finally, an old gentleman in the balcony smiled and nodded his head. Only then did the youth's face beam with joy. You see, the cheers of the crowd meant nothing until he had the approval of the master!

If God values us, then that's all that matters. Other people's opinions are unimportant. Other people's criticism and ridicule are unimportant. Other people's admiration and flattery are unimportant. Robert Browning wrote in his 1864 dramatic monologue "Rabbi Ben Ezra," "All I could never be. All men ignored in me. This, I was worth to God." That's what gives us value.

How can we realize this wonderful gift from God? How can we feel valued and then pass on that gift to others? We must believe that Jesus offers not only life, but abundant life! And abundant life includes value!

Security

One of our most basic human needs is the need for security. Fear and uncertainty destroy us. A Japanese soldier on Guam spent twenty-eight years in a prison of fear. When American forces arrived, he ran into the jungle and hid. He later heard that the war was over by reading a leaflet that was dropped. Still, he was so insecure that he stayed in his cave.

For over a quarter of a century, he came out only at night. He existed on frogs, rats, and mangoes. Finally, some hunters convinced him that it was safe to leave the jungle.

People said, "What a waste of life, being so afraid that he ceased to live."

Yes, it's a waste, and it's shocking, but it's also very common.

Negative Effects of Insecurity

The negative effects of insecurity are serious. We don't grow or learn or serve or produce fruit when we're nervous and unsure. Unfortunately, everyone is unsure at times. Everyone has anxiety and crises and trauma. No one lives a pain-free life. Paul expressed it well, saying, "Our bodies had no rest, but we were afflicted in every way—disputes without and fears within" (2 Cor 7:5).

Such insecurities are really the root of all evil. Insecure people are like the man with the one talent who hid it in the ground. He was reluctant to try because he was afraid his master would punish him for failure. But Jesus condemned him as an unfaithful servant (see Matt 25:24–28).

Also, insecure people are prone to follow any con artist or charismatic leader who comes along simply because they don't want to take personal responsibility for their own behavior. But perhaps the most destructive thing about insecure people is their critical and judgmental attitudes. Since they don't feel adequate, they play the "seesaw" game. They try to put themselves up by putting others down. They hope God is grading on the curve and will therefore overlook their flaws if they can make someone else look worse.

It's obvious that most hostility and prejudice and even violence stem from fear. Insecure people become overly defensive and even paranoid. Every shadow becomes an enemy. A pastor told of walking through a new building project. The staff and the construction crew had left, and it was getting late. He tiptoed over the debris and noticed a room he'd never entered before.

When he walked in, it was dark, and he waited for his eyes to adjust. That's when he saw the other man in the room with him. He said, "Sir, can I help you?" But the stranger didn't answer. That's when the pastor noticed that this person looked very unpleasant, so he repeated, "What are you doing here?" The man still didn't reply. The pastor began to think he was in serious trouble, so he reached for the door. When he did, he realized he wasn't in the room with another man at all. He was in the room with a mirror.

That's what happens to us when we're insecure. We become our own worst enemy. We second-guess our actions. We hesitate over decisions. We doubt our salvation. We miss the joy God offers. Jesus came to give us abundant life, and no one can enjoy an abundant life without security.

Positive Effects of Security

Security is one of the most precious and productive benefits of the gospel. In fact, security is essential for an abundant life because there are many positive effects of security.

Secure people are opposite to insecure people. If we're secure, we can try different things and feel free to take risks because we know God will understand if we fail. We aren't tempted to follow gurus like Jim Jones because we have a perfect leader to guide our lives. We don't have to wear masks and hide flaws and deny weaknesses because we know God loves us unconditionally!

Absolute assurance is one of the greatest blessings of our faith. Jesus promised total security: "'I give them eternal life, and they will never perish. No one will snatch them out of my hand. What my Father has given me is greater than all else, and no can snatch it out of my Father's hand'" (John 10:28–29).

Secure people can enjoy daily life. Jesus tells us God knows our needs (see Luke 12:29–32). In fact, "Do not be anxious!" is not a mild suggestion. It's a command! Jesus said, "Do not worry about your life, what you will eat or what you will drink, or about your body, what you will wear. Is not life more than food, and the body more than clothing?... But strive first for the kingdom of God and his righteousness, and all these things will be given to you as well" (Matt 6:25, 33).

Secure people can even face an uncertain future because Jesus said, "Do not worry about tomorrow" (Matt 6:34). Always dreading a recession or loss of a job or an earthquake is useless fear that destroys our happiness and productivity. Jesus wasn't saying we should not prepare for problems; he never advocated an irresponsible or lazy lifestyle. But to live day after day distracted with worry wastes both time and energy. It also limits our ability to serve and takes a heavy toll on our health.

A Florida couple looked out their window and saw that the ground beneath the street had literally collapsed, creating a sinkhole. Tumbling into the ever-deepening pit were automobiles, sidewalks, and lawn furniture. The building itself would be the next to go.

Sinkholes occur when underground streams drain away during seasons of drought, causing the ground at the surface to lose its support. Suddenly, everything simply caves in, leaving people with a terrifying suspicion that nothing, not even the earth beneath their feet, is trustworthy.

We can't live like that. God knows we need to feel secure. That's why *fear not* is one of the most common phrases in the Bible. People who are secure have a permanent feeling of calm assurance. Security helps us experience abundant life!

How to Realize Security

If all of us have such a desperate need for security, then how can we realize it in our daily lives? We are fortunate as Christians because the scriptures give us many promises concerning security.

The psalmist said, "I will both lie down and sleep in peace; for you alone, O LORD, make me lie down in safety" (Ps 4:8). Later, he said, "Even though I walk through the darkest valley, I fear no evil; for you are with me; your rod and your staff—they comfort me" (Ps 23:4). Then he said, "God is our refuge and strength, a very present help in trouble" (Ps 46:1).

In times of crises, we can remember that God is with us. Paul said, "Who will separate us from the love of Christ? Will hardship, or distress, or persecution, or famine, or nakedness, or peril, or sword?... No, in all these things we are more than conquerors through him who loved us. For I am convinced that neither death, nor life, nor angels, nor rulers, nor things present, nor things to come, nor powers, nor height, nor depth, nor anything else in all creation, will be able to separate us from the love of God in Christ Jesus our Lord" (see Rom 8:35–39).

It's reassuring to know that even very bad things can be redeemed. Our failures can be learning experiences. Our sins can teach us humility. Our sorrows can make us appreciative and empathetic. That's what Paul meant when he said, "We know that all things work together for good for those who love God, who are called according to his purpose" (Rom 8:28).

You see, God doesn't change external circumstances. Instead, he changes internal conditions. A new father recounted, "One night, we left our little son in the nursery and went to bed. Soon, there was a tremendous crash of thunder right above us. I heard the baby scream. I ran to his room. I just knew a tree had fallen or a window had been smashed, but thankfully he was just frightened by the noise. After I picked him up, held him close, and talked softly, he became quieter and began to relax. Now, I didn't do a thing to calm the storm that raged without. Instead, I was able to calm the storm that raged within."

It's the same with us. God doesn't still the storms without by stopping wars and crime and natural disasters. Instead, he stills the storms within us. Christ promised us his peace in the midst of a troubled world, saying, "Peace I leave with you…. Do not let your hearts be troubled, and do not let them be afraid" (John 14:27).

As Christians, we are members of God's family, and a child's relationship is permanently established by his birth. A misbehaving child is not kicked out of the family. Failure does not cancel his status. Mistakes don't nullify his welcome. In "The Death of the Hired Man," Robert Frost wrote, "A family is the place where, when you have to go there, they have to take you in!"

An old story illustrates our absolute security as God's child. Once, a preacher boarded a bus and sat down beside a young man. They rode in silence for a while, but the youth seemed so nervous that the preacher said, "Son, I'm a minister. Can I help you?"

Finally, the boy answered, "Yes, sir! I've got to talk to someone. You see, about two years ago, I got drunk, hit my dad, and left. For the past two years I've been in all kinds of trouble. But last week I accepted Christ. The first thing I thought of was my parents. I wrote a letter and said, 'Dad, if you still consider me your son, I'd like to come back home.' I explained that I'd be on this bus and if he wanted me to get off, I would."

The preacher was confused and said, "Son, how are you going to know whether your dad wants you?"

The young man replied, "Preacher, our house is right by this highway, and there's an old apple tree in the front yard. I told my dad that if they still loved me, just to have a white cloth in that old tree and I'd get off."

Then tears came as the boy said, "Preacher, I'm almost there, but I'm afraid to look. What if they don't want me?"

The preacher said, "That's all right. I'll look for you."

Soon, a big smile came over his face, and he said, "Son, you don't have a thing to worry about. There are white cloths hanging all over that old apple tree. And that's not all. Your mom and dad are out in the yard waving a big white bedsheet."

This is our story. No matter what we've done, no matter how long we've strayed, that's how God will respond to us!

How can we realize this wonderful gift? How can we feel secure and then pass that gift on to others? To do this we must believe that Jesus offers us not only life, but abundant life! And abundant life includes security.

Forgiveness

One of the most basic human needs is the need for forgiveness. Queen Victoria once paid a visit to a paper mill. The foreman who showed her around didn't know who she was. In the sorting shop, she was told that when the rags were separated from the city garbage, they would make the finest white paper. After she left, the foreman found out who she was. A few weeks later, her majesty received a package of the most delicate white stationery with the queen's likeness for a watermark. A note told her it was made from the dirty rags she had inspected. That illustrates Christ's work in us as he makes us into new creatures.

Negative Effects of Guilt

The negative effects of guilt are destructive. Every person needs forgiveness. All of us are born with instincts that include self-preservation, selfishness, and natural hostilities. That's what some theologians call "original sin." These animalistic tendencies must be overcome. As soon as we become autonomous and begin making choices, all of us make errors in judgment. All of us develop addictions and bad habits. In short, all of us have guilts.

An old urban legend holds that Sir Arthur Conan Doyle told of playing a practical joke on twelve people who were in positions of fame and power. He sent a telegram that said, "Flee at once; all is discovered." Within twenty-four hours all twelve of the so-called virtuous men had left the country .

That's what guilt can do! Furthermore, people who feel guilty almost always become judgmental of others. They project their own shame and distress onto everyone around them. They try to justify their own problems by showing that others are worse. Such a burden of humiliation and regret can destroy us.

A speaker picked up a glass of water and asked, "How heavy is this?" Answers were called out, ranging from 20 to 500 grams. The lecturer replied, "The absolute weight doesn't matter. It depends on how long I try to hold it. If I hold it for a minute, that's not a problem. If I hold it for an hour, I'll have an ache in my right arm. If I hold it for a day, you'll have to call an ambulance. In each case it's the same weight, but the longer I hold it, the heavier it becomes."

The same thing is true of us. Guilt is useful to warn us of danger, but if we continue to carry our burden of guilt, sooner or later it becomes so increasingly heavy that we won't be able to bear it. God knows this! That's why he forgives and forgets. A minister once carried a secret burden. He had committed a serious sin many years before, during his college days. No one knew what he had done, but they did know he had repented. Even so, he suffered years of remorse without any sense of God's forgiveness.

A woman in his congregation claimed to have visions in which Jesus spoke to her. The minister, skeptical of her claims, said, "The next time you speak to the Lord, just ask him what sin I committed as a youth."

The woman agreed. When she came to the church a few days later, the minister asked, "Did he visit you?"

"Yes."

"And did you ask him what sin I committed in college?"

"Yes, I asked him," she replied.

"Well, what did he say?"

"He said, 'My child, I don't remember.'"

In fact, that's a biblical promise: "I will be merciful toward their iniquities, and I will remember their sins no more" (Heb 8:12).

Paul would have become mentally ill if he had dwelt on his past persecution of the church and participation in the murder of Steven and other Christians. Instead, he said, "One thing I do: forgetting what lies behind and straining forward to what lies ahead, I press on toward the goal" (Phil 3:13–14).

Forgiveness is essential for abundant life. Jesus came to give us abundant life, and no one can enjoy abundant life without forgiveness.

Positive Effects of Forgiveness

Forgiveness is an important theme of the gospel because there are many positive effects of forgiveness. In fact, forgiveness is essential for abundant life.

Jesus offers a life that rises above our unproductive traits and practices. Our attitudes can change, and our faults and mistakes can be forgiven. In fact, Jesus absolutely abolishes guilt. He said, "Very truly, I tell you, anyone who hears my word and believes him who sent me has eternal life, and does not come under judgment, but has passed from death to life" (John 5:24).

His offers of forgiveness were a constant and definite part of his ministry. He didn't condemn the woman caught in the act of adultery. When the crowd hauled her before him and shouted condemnation, he said, "'Let anyone among you who is without sin be the first to throw a stone at her.'... Jesus was left alone with the woman standing before him. Jesus straightened up and said to her, 'Woman, where are they? Has no one condemned you?' She said, 'No one, sir.' And Jesus said, 'Neither do I condemn you'" (see John 8:7–11).

The only hands without stones that day were the Lord's. In fact, Jesus specialized in forgiving sinners. He even offered forgiveness to those who crucified him: "When they came to the place called The Skull, they crucified Jesus there.... Jesus said, 'Father, forgive them; for they do not know what they are doing'" (Luke 23:33–34).

He knew forgiveness is essential. When questioned about our relationship with each other, Jesus said, "[You must forgive] not seven times, but, I tell you, seventy-seven times" (Matt 18:22). He knew that people who feel forgiven have inner peace and therefore have no need to project their own flaws and faults and mistakes onto their associates.

God promises total removal of all sins. He uses dramatic analogies to describe this divine action: "I have swept away your transgressions like a cloud, and your sins like mist" (Isa 44:22).

God even overrides our own feelings when we can't forgive ourselves: "And by this we will know that we are from the truth and will reassure our hearts before him whenever our hearts condemn us; for God is greater than our hearts, and he knows everything" (1 John 3:19–20).

Forgiveness helps us experience an abundant life!

How to Realize Forgiveness

If all of us have such a desperate need for forgiveness, then how can we realize it in our daily lives? We are fortunate as Christians because the scriptures give us many promises concerning forgiveness.

The psalmist said, "As far as the east is from the west, so far he removes our transgressions from us" (Ps 103:12).

Isaiah said, "The seraph touched my mouth...and said, 'Now that this has touched your lips, your guilt has departed and your sin is blotted out'" (Isa 6:7).

Jeremiah said, "I will forgive their iniquity, and remember their sin no more" (Jer 31:34).

Paul quoted a psalm, saying, "Blessed are those whose iniquities are forgiven, and whose sins are covered; blessed is the one against whom the Lord will not reckon sin" (Rom 4:7–8).

The writer of Hebrews said, "Let us approach with a true heart in full assurance of faith, with our hearts sprinkled clean from an evil conscience" (Heb 10:22).

John said, "If we confess our sins, he who is faithful and just and will forgive us our sins and cleanse us from all unrighteousness" (1 John 1:9).

When we believe these many promises of grace, we can begin to forgive ourselves for our past problems. We can deal with our mistakes and rest assured that God has forgiven us and erased our guilt. We can understand that every saint has a past and every sinner has a future.

Let's consider a spiritual analogy. A new Christian said, "I see myself at the last judgment, and, as at an earthly trial, my identity has to be established. But there is an interruption. The Supreme Judge has hardly put to me the question, 'Who are you?' before my satanic accuser breaks in and answers for me, 'Who is he, you ask? I will tell you. He is the one who has done such and such, and failed to do such and such. He has ignored the plight of his neighbors. He has been silent when he ought to have confessed. The gifts you have given him have not made him humble but proud.' The accuser continued with his accusation. But then the Son of God, who is counsel for the defense, interrupts. 'O, Father and Judge,' he says, 'the prosecutor has spoken the truth. This man has done all these things. But the accusation is without substance. For he is no longer what he was!' And although the judge knows very well what Christ is saying, for the sake of the audience he asks, 'Who is he then if he is no longer what he was?' To this Christ replies, 'He has become my disciple and believed me that you want to be his father, as you are mine. Hence, I have canceled his past and nailed the accusations to my cross. Therefore, since this person has accepted me and gained the right of sonship that you promised, look upon him as you look upon me. He is my brother and your son.'"

Now, this is the story of our forgiveness. Paul said, "[God erased] the record that stood against us with its legal demands. He set this aside, nailing it to the cross" (Col 2:14).

How can we realize this wonderful gift from God? How can we feel forgiveness and then pass that gift to others? To do this we must believe that Jesus offers us not only life, but abundant life! And abundant life includes forgiveness.

Guidance

One of our most basic human needs is the need for guidance. Few of us are absolutely sure about our direction in life. Some of you may have seen the bumper sticker that reads, "Don't follow me; I'm lost." Then there was a sign on a narrow road that read, "Dead end." A stubborn motorist took it anyway and had to turn around. When he did, he faced another sign that read in huge letters, "Welcome back, stupid."

Following directions and knowing what to believe is difficult. It can feel like drowning. I'm sure most of us have felt this way at times.

Negative Effects of Confusion

The negative effects of confusion are well known. Everybody needs advice and guidance as they make decisions in life. We can't know everything. We can't see the big picture. We can't always look into the future and realize the long-term results or the far-reaching consequences of our actions.

Suppose you're following a slow-moving car. Should you pass? Well, if it's going to turn at the next corner, the answer is "No!" However, if it's going to continue at this speed for the next 100 miles, the answer is "Yes!" But you don't know at this point. Other more momentous choices are just as uncertain. Life is a series of problematic episodes.

Research shows that we make over 200 decisions a day: what to wear, what to eat, what to do, what to say. Over and over, we select and choose. Furthermore, options are increasing at an alarming rate. More brands, more merchandise, more ads—it's overwhelming. Then there are the crucial, once-in-a-lifetime decisions about mates, occupations, and education. Like Robert Frost said in "The Road Not Taken," we can stand looking at a fork in the road in a paralyzing dilemma of which to follow. After choosing one, Frost says:

> Two roads diverged in a wood, and I—
> I took the one less traveled by,
> And that has made all the difference.

Yes, what we decide today will make a difference in the future. But how do we know what to do? Unless we have spiritual guidance, we may be indecisive and hesitant. Elijah spoke to this problem when he said, "'How long will you go limping with two different opinions? If the LORD is God, follow him; but if Baal, then follow him'" (1 Kgs 18:21).

But sometimes instead of hesitancy we do the opposite by making a lot of mistakes and wasting a lot of time using trial-and-error procedures. One third of all American workers changed jobs last year. Even the average pastor stays at a church for less than two years. Jeremiah spoke to folks like that when he said, "How lightly you gad about, changing your ways!" (Jer 2:36).

Instead of doing their best where they are and blooming where they are planted, too many people get bored and constantly seek greener pastures. Such restlessness and perplexity and uncertainty ruins our lives and our relationships. It also makes us vulnerable to unwise leadership. Manipulators deliberately deceive us. In the days before electronic navigation, lighthouses served as guides for ships. Many pirates purposely caused shipwrecks by setting up false lights on hazardous coastlines. By trusting in these false lights, ships would crash on the rocks. Then pirates would collect the cargo and leave the crew to drown.

Other leaders are honest but mistaken. At a military funeral one preacher who was to lead the procession unfortunately picked the wrong door. As a result the honor guard marched with military precision into a broom closet and had to beat a hasty retreat. If you're going to follow, make sure you are following someone who knows where he's going.

Jesus came to give us abundant life, and no one can enjoy an abundant life without guidance.

Positive Effects of Guidance

Guidance is an important theme of the gospel because there are many positive effects of guidance. In fact, guidance is essential for an abundant life. Jesus knew this. Therefore, he left us instructions and advice: "'The words that I have spoken to you are spirit and life'" (John 6:63).

"'If you love me, you will keep my commandments'" (John 14:15).

He also said, "'Blessed...are those who hear the word of God and obey it!'" (Luke 11:28).

Then he gave us an example to follow, explaining, "'My sheep hear my voice. I know them, and they follow me'" (John 10:27).

Later, he said, "'I have set you an example, that you should do as I have done to you'" (John 13:15).

But the greatest gift Jesus gave us was an internal moral compass. He said, "'I still have many things to say to you, but you cannot bear them now.

When the Spirit of truth comes, he will guide you into all the truth…. [The Spirit] will take what is mine and declare it to you'" (see John 16:12–13, 15).

Tuning in to that truth is very important. A guide at Yellowstone National Park was leading a group of tourists to a certain lookout point. He was so intent on telling the hikers about the flowers and animals that he turned off his two-way radio. Nearing the tower, the group was met by a breathless ranger, who asked why he hadn't responded to his messages. You see, a grizzly bear had been observed stalking the group, and the authorities were trying to warn them of the danger.

Any time we tune out God's guidance, we put ourselves and others at risk.

A sense of guidance gives us confidence. Once, a man got lost in the woods. For hours he circled in the tangled underbrush, vainly seeking a landmark. Everywhere he turned, masses of unfamiliar greenery increased his confusion. Finally, just as the sun was setting, he stumbled through a bramble thicket and saw a familiar landmark. Instantly, he knew where he was. He still had a long walk ahead, but now he had his bearings.

God gives us such landmarks to guide us. These landmarks include scriptural admonitions; They include asking, "What would Jesus do?" They include worshiping at church. They include prayer and meditation. They include relying on our consciences and intuition.

It's encouraging to know that God knows the end from the beginning: "I am God, and there is no one like me, declaring the end from the beginning" (Isa 46:9–10).

Guidance is important because it helps us avoid dangerous and destructive mistakes. It gives us confidence and assurance and leads to peace and success. Guidance helps us experience an abundant life!

How to Realize and Receive Guidance

If all of us have such a desperate need for guidance, then how can we realize it in our daily lives? We are fortunate as Christians because the scriptures give us many promises concerning guidance. Paul told Timothy, "From childhood you have known the sacred writings that are able to instruct you" (2 Tim 3:15).

God declared, "I am the LORD your God, who teaches you for your own good, who leads you in the way you should go" (Isa 48:17).

He also said, "When you turn to the right or when you turn to the left, your ears shall hear a word behind you, saying, 'This is the way; walk in it'" (Isa 30:21).

The psalmist said, "He leads the humble in what is right, and teaches the humble in his way" (Ps 25:9).

James said, "If any of you is lacking wisdom, ask God, who gives to all generously and ungrudgingly, and it will be given you" (Jas 1:5).

God also speaks through creation. The psalmist said, "The heavens are telling the glory of God, and the firmament proclaims his handiwork.... There is no speech, nor are there words; their voice is not heard; yet their voice goes out through all the earth" (see Ps 19:1–4).

God speaks through prayer. Jeremiah said, "Let the LORD your God show us where we should go and what we should do" (Jer 42:3).

God speaks through people. Paul told Timothy to "set the believers an example in speech and conduct, in love, in faith, in purity" (1 Tim 4:12).

God speaks through our conscience and our intellect. Paul said, "They must hold fast to the mystery of the faith with a clear conscience" (1 Tim 3:9).

He also said, "Let all be fully convinced in their own minds" (Rom 14:5).

All of these methods are valuable. But we must be connected and tuned in to God before we can be guided.

A certain species of ant lives in Africa. The queen and the young are sheltered in large tunnels. The worker ants go on lengthy foraging trips to gather food for the colony. While on these long trips, in a way not yet understood by scientists, the workers are constantly oriented to the queen. If the queen is disturbed, the distant worker ants become jittery and confused. If this connection is lost, they rush about helter-skelter until they die in the field.

This is a picture of human beings who lose their spiritual connection. It's important to remember that we need guidance every day, because small mistakes can become disastrous mistakes. But we need guidance even more when we face momentous life decisions. If we are uncertain, we must wait for divine counsel. The psalmist said, "Make me to know your ways, O LORD; teach me your paths. Lead me in your truth.... Wait for the LORD, and keep to his way" (Pss 25:4–5; 37:34).

Poet Annie Johnson Flint wrote about God's guidance to those who need it in "The Red Sea Place":

> He will send the wind, He will heap the floods,
> When He says to your soul, "Go on."[1]

How can we realize this wonderful gift from God? How can we feel his guidance and pass on that gift to others? To do this we must believe that Jesus offers us not only life, but abundant life. And abundant life includes guidance!

Note

[1] *He Giveth More Grace*, (Hayden Press: 2019) 41.

Support

Some first graders were telling what they wanted to be when they grew up. Each child announced, "I'd like to be a nurse," or "I want to be a farmer." The last child to speak was the shyest little boy in the class. He announced, "I'm going to be a lion tamer. I'll get in a cage full of fierce animals with my whip and chair. I'll make them jump through hoops."

Suddenly, in the midst of this exciting tale, he saw his classmates staring at him with open mouths. They couldn't believe him! Quickly he added, "Of course, my daddy will be with me." He was right. None of us can tame lions without support.

Negative Effects of Lack of Support

No one is totally adequate for every situation. People without support and assistance either get discouraged and give up or become bitter and resentful. No one can go it alone. Take, for example, a man who believed himself to be the finest musician in the world. Accordingly, when the curtain went up for a symphonic concert, the audience was astonished to see seventy empty chairs, with the appropriate instruments, and only this one person to play them all. When the conductor's baton signaled the start, this man ran frantically from one instrument to another, trying to keep up with the conductor.

This may be a ridiculous allegory, but people who try to live their lives without support are almost in that position. It's not a sign of weakness to need help. Paul said, "Not that we are competent of ourselves to claim anything as coming from us; our competence is from God" (2 Cor 3:5).

Life is hard. There are personal problems, relationship problems, professional problems, financial problems, and moral problems. Then there is a lot of pressure for success. Failure is a terrible word, but for Christians failure is never final. The psalmist said, "Though we stumble, we shall not fall headlong, for the LORD holds us by the hand" (Ps 37:24).

Micah said, "When I fall, I shall rise" (Mic 7:8).

Most of you have heard of "Murphy's law," which says, "Anything that *can* go wrong, will go wrong." But just as the law of aerodynamics supersedes the law of gravity in lifting jets into the air, so Christ's law of grace lifts us above Murphy's law.

A minister on an airplane was talking to a young man who said he was a Christian, but he didn't know how much longer he could stand up against his temptations. At that the minister took a pencil out of his pocket and said, "I'm going to make this pencil stand on end on this table in spite of the turbulence on this plane." The youth thought there was some trick involved and said, "I'm afraid that won't be easy, sir."

"But, look, I'm doing it now."

"Oh, but you're holding it up," retorted his fellow passenger.

"Of course I'm holding it," the minister replied. "Who ever heard of a pencil standing on its end without being held?"

The young man smiled. "So you mean I can't stand alone; I need the support of my heavenly Father?"

Scripture says, "I will strengthen you, I will help you, I will uphold you with my victorious right hand" (Isa 41:10).

Positive Effects of Support

Jesus promised, "I am with you always, to the end of the age" (Matt 28:20). We can be absolutely sure about God's support. When someone asked a Christian, "Aren't you afraid you will slip through God's fingers?," he replied, "No! I am one of his fingers." Every believer is a part of the body of Christ, and the church symbolizes that body.

There's a story about two apple blossoms named Annie and Abby. They were admired for their beauty and aroma. One day, a lady cut Abby off the tree and put her in a vase. Both blossoms still looked identical, but there was a fundamental difference. Abby was now on her own, cut off from her support. She soon turned into an ugly brown twig. Annie, however, continued to receive life from the tree and produced an apple.

That's our story. If we cut ourselves off from our spiritual roots, we'll wither. Jesus said, "The branch bear fruit by itself unless it abides in the vine.... I am the vine, you are the branches. Those who abide in me and I in them bear much fruit, because apart from me you can do nothing. Whoever does not abide in me is thrown away like a branch and withers" (see John 15:4–6). The church provides that spiritual connection by keeping us in tune with God and other believers. People who feel supported and assisted can overcome obstacles and live productive lives.

A Sunday school teacher decided to have her class memorize Psalm 23. Little Ricky was excited about this task, but he just couldn't remember the words. After much practice, he could barely get past the first line. On the day that the children were scheduled to recite in front of the congregation, Ricky was very nervous. When it was his turn, he stepped up to the microphone and said proudly, "The Lord is my shepherd, and that's all I need to know!" Similarly, Paul said, "My God will satisfy every need of yours according to his riches in glory in Christ Jesus" (Phil 4:19).

Yes, God gives us strength, but he doesn't do our jobs for us. He knows we must learn some things for ourselves by trial and error. The child taking her first steps holds on, then lets go, then falls, then struggles to her feet for another attempt. No one has discovered another way to learn to walk.

Support helps us grow and develop.

How to Realize and Accept Support

If all of us have such a desperate need for support, then how can we realize it in our daily lives? We are fortunate as Christians because the scriptures give us many promises concerning support.

Isaiah said, "He gives power to the faint, and strengthens the powerless.... Those who wait for the LORD shall renew their strength, they shall mount up with wings like eagles, they shall run and not be weary, they shall walk and not faint" (Isa 40:29, 31).

Paul said, "Be strong in the Lord and in the strength of his power" (Eph 6:10). He also said, "I can do all things through him who strengthens me" (Phil 4:13).

The writer of Hebrews said, "Let us therefore approach the throne of grace with boldness, so that we may receive mercy and find grace to help in time of need" (Heb 4:16).

God strengthens us by presence, teachings, and by working through other believers. As a church we are here to encourage, assist, and support each other.

As Christians we can depend upon each other for support, and we can depend on God. All of us face hardships, obstacles, and sorrows. We can identify with the sailor who stood at the helm trying to guide his craft through turbulent waters. As he lost his direction, he cried out, "Oh, God, the sea is so great, and my boat is so small!" Fortunately, for us, God is in our boat with us.

How can we realize this wonderful gift from God? How can we feel supported and then pass on that gift to others? To do this we must believe that Jesus offers us not only life, but abundant life! And that abundant life includes support.

Purpose

One of the most basic human needs is the need for purpose. Many years ago, a woman took her first journey on a train. She sat down and began fumbling with the window to be sure she got exactly the right amount of air. She pulled the window shade up and down to adjust the light. She worked with her baggage to get it placed just right. Then she took out her mirror and comb and fussed with her hair. Just about the time she got everything fixed, the conductor called out her station. "Oh, my," she said, "if I had known the trip was going to be so short, I wouldn't have wasted so much time on trifles."

It's the same with us. Our life journey is too short to be wasted on trifles.

Negative Effects of Aimlessness

The negative effects of aimlessness are disastrous. Every person needs a purpose in life. People without a purpose waste their lives. They are unfocused, easily distracted, and aimless. They seek satisfaction in dangerous and destructive pursuits and never accomplish anything.

There was once a dog named Rex who spotted a bear and gave chase. As he ran, however, a fox crossed his path. Rex turned his attention away from the bear and began to chase the fox. As he raced within a few yards of the fox, a rabbit jumped out from a bush, and Rex forgot the fox and began to chase it. Rex was really tired, but he kept running. But as Rex was just about to catch the rabbit, a mouse came by. Rex turned again and began to chase the mouse. Through brambles and thickets they went. But just as Rex was about to catch the mouse, it disappeared down a hole. Tired and scratched up, Rex stood over the hole and barked. Then, finally, he collapsed in exhaustion. Rex lacked purpose.

Are we like that—jumping from one fad to another and achieving nothing? Then there are other people who "dream" through life and end up empty and frustrated. Is your life a disillusionment and a disappointment? The writer of Ecclesiastes felt this way when he exclaimed, "Vanity of vanities! All is vanity" (Eccl 1:2).

But life doesn't have to be meaningless. Remember, life is God's gift to us. What we do with it is our gift to God. Later, the writer of Ecclesiastes became more focused and said, "Enjoy life with the wife whom you love…. Whatever your hand finds to do, do with your might" (Eccl 9:9–10).

Jesus came to give us abundant life, and no one can enjoy an abundant life without purpose.

Positive Effects of Purpose

Purpose is an important theme of the gospel because there are many positive effects of purpose. In fact, purpose is essential for an abundant life. It's not what you are nor what you have been that God sees. It's what you are meant to be!

Jesus lived a life of purpose. He said, "'My food is to do the will of him who sent me and to complete his work" (John 4:34). Jesus knew his purpose, and he was focused on his goal. That's the only way we can accomplish anything.

Suppose you went to a friend's house and found him working diligently using wood, nails, a hammer, and a saw. After watching him work for some time, you asked, "What are you building?" If he responded "I don't know," you would probably think it was very odd that he would be building something without an end in sight.

We were created for a purpose, and it's our job to discover that purpose.

Jesus stressed service to others: "The king will answer them, 'Truly I tell you, just as you did it to one of the least of these who are members of my family, you did it to me'" (Matt 25:40).

He gave a specific commission to every believer: "Go therefore and make disciples of all nations…teaching them to obey everything that I have commanded you" (Matt 28:19–20).

Louis Pasteur was the pioneer of immunology. Pasteur worked for years on a rabies vaccine and was ready to begin experimenting on himself when a nine-year-old boy, Joseph Meister, who had been bitten by a rabid dog was brought to him for help. Pasteur gave Joseph ten daily injections, and the boy lived.[1] Likewise, our greatest legacy will be those who live eternally because of our efforts.

People with purpose are motivated to achieve greatness. They are careful to finish projects, and they are able to enjoy fulfillment. Dr. Alfredo Quiño-nes-Hinojsa seeks a cure for brain cancer with the same determination that has shaped every facet of his life. As a teenager he climbed a fence along the border between Mexico and the United States. The first time he was caught and returned, but just hours later he climbed again. That time he made it.

An undocumented immigrant, Quinones spoke no English and had no money. He labored on a farm, until one day a cousin said that working on a farm was all he would ever do.

Quinones didn't agree. He enrolled at a community college while juggling jobs as a painter and welder. He won a scholarship to the University of California. From there, he went on to medical school at Harvard and became a citizen. Now, his office walls are covered in awards. He's a man with a purpose.[2]

Purpose helps us experience an abundant life.

How to Realize Purpose

If all of us have such a desperate need for purpose, then how can we realize it in our daily lives? We are fortunate as Christians because the scriptures give us many promises concerning purpose. Jeremiah explains that each of us has a special mission in life: "'For surely I know the plans I have for you,' says the LORD, 'plans for your welfare and not for harm, to give you a future with hope'" (Jer 29:11).

Paul said, "We know that all things work together for good for those who love God, who are called according to his purpose" (Rom 8:28).

Later he said, "Therefore, my beloved, be steadfast, immovable, always excelling in the work of the Lord, because you know that in the Lord your labor is not in vain" (1 Cor 15:58).

Paul stressed God's plan for us when he said, "Render service with enthusiasm, as to the Lord and not to men and women, knowing that whatever good we do, we will receive the same again from the Lord" (see Eph 6:7–8).

"Whatever your task, put yourselves into it, as done for the Lord and not for your masters, since you know that from the Lord you will receive the inheritance as your reward; you serve the Lord Christ" (Col 3:23–24).

There is no excuse for apathy and idleness. Everyone can do something. God created us, saved us, called us, and commissioned us for service. He has a purpose for our lives.

Sometimes we miss our calling and waste time on detours. James Whistler and Carl Sandburg both failed as students at West Point. They were not able to make it in the military, yet each eventually found his niche and his purpose. Whistler became a famous artist, and Sandburg became a famous poet!

God doesn't create junk. God doesn't waste resources. God doesn't make mistakes. He didn't give you life, time, and abilities without a purpose.

No one else will ever be able to fill the role God planned for you. It's your responsibility to find and fill that role.

A tiny acorn has the potential to become a great oak tree. It's the same with us. Each of us has great potential. How can we realize this wonderful gift from God? How can we find our purpose and then use it to enrich others? In order to do this, we must believe that Jesus offers us not only life, but abundant life. And abundant life includes purpose.

[1]Dr. Howard Markel, "Louis Pasteur's risky move to save a boy from almost certain death," *PBS News Hour*, https://www.pbs.org/newshour/health/louis-pasteurs-risky-move-to-save-a-boy-from-almost-certain-death, July 7, 2016.

[2]"The Story of Dr. Alfredo Quiñones-Hinojsa," https://www.doctorqmd.com/my-story.html, Q, accessed August 5, 2021.

Hope

Negative Effects of Despair

The negative effects of despair are devastating. Shakespeare's Macbeth describes a hopeless existence with these words: "Tomorrow and tomorrow and tomorrow creeps in its petty pace from day to day."

People without hope are miserable and desperate, and nothing matters. They are apathetic and nonproductive. A small town in England had the tradition of a party where all the children received gifts. It was a festive occasion that included bright smiles of youngsters, a tall tree in the square, and colorful packages. Unfortunately, an evil gang decided to play a cruel joke on one youngster.

As the pile of gifts became smaller and smaller, this child's face became sadder and sadder. His heart was heavy as he watched everyone else receive presents. Then someone came to him with a gift. His was the last one under the tree. His eyes danced as he looked at the beautifully wrapped package. His excitement soared as he tore away the ribbons. His fingers raced to rip away the paper. But as he opened the box, his heart sank. It was empty!

The packaging was attractive. The ribbons were colorful. But when he got to the inside, the box was empty!

Are we like that? Has life played a cruel trick on us? Are we disillusioned? Have we been lied to? Do we feel cheated? Have others forgotten their promises and failed to live up to their agreements? Have we become cynical and embittered, unable to trust and afraid to care?

Well, life is hard, and there are two types of hope. People who live on passive hope dream of riches and miracles and a good fairy to reward them. It's their way of enduring the harshness of reality. While people with active hope use their strength and imagination to make their dreams come true, people with passive hope watch with admiration the pioneers building cities and bridges and hospitals and kindergartens while they themselves do nothing. People with active hope continue to build those cities and bridges and hospitals and kindergartens. Paul said, "We have heard of your faith in Christ Jesus and of the love that you have for all the saints, because of the hope laid up for you in heaven" (Col 1:4–5).

If we believe in an infinite God, there is always more. In medieval times sculptors at the Strait of Gibraltar carved the words "Ne plus ultra"—which means "nothing beyond"—into the cliff that overlooks the ocean. That was it! That was as far as man could go. They were content to let their world end at this point. But for at least one man, it was not enough! After Columbus did the impossible and discovered the new world, workmen removed the "Ne." Now it reads "Plus ultra," or "more beyond." That should be the motto of Christianity. God assures us that no matter where we go, no matter how far we reach out in any direction, there is always "more beyond."

God blesses active hope. Furthermore, he offers eternal hope. Jesus came to give us abundant life, and no one can enjoy abundant life without hope.

Positive Effects of Hope

Hope is an important theme of the gospel because there are many positive effects of hope. In fact, hope is essential for an abundant life.

Jesus epitomizes hope. He promises the kind of life where our desires can be realized and our hopes can materialize. He described great joy: "I have said these things to you so that my joy may be in you, and that your joy may be complete" (John 15:11).

He emphasized that small deeds will be remembered: "For truly I tell you, whoever gives you a cup of water to drink because you bear the name of Christ will by no means lose the reward" (Mark 9:41).

He promised great things: "His master said to him, 'Well done, good and trustworthy slave; you have been trustworthy in a few things, I will put you in charge of many things; enter into the joy of your master'" (Matt 25:21).

He described a bright future: "'Do not let your hearts be troubled. Believe in God, believe also in me. In my Father's house there are many dwelling places. If it were not so, would I have told you that I go to prepare a place for you? And if I go and prepare a place for you, I will come again and will take you to myself, so that where I am, there you may be also" (John 14:1–3).

Paul said, "The creation waits with eager longing for the revealing of the children of God" (Rom 8:19).

Without the power of hope, the world would be a different place. Military campaigns would have ended differently. George Washington, surveying his ragged forces at Valley Forge, would have surrendered. So would Winston Churchill in the early days of 1941. Thomas Alva Edison, after testing thousands of possible filaments for an electric light, would have shrugged and said, "I give up. Nobody will ever figure this out."

Hope is powerful. Without hope people give up. They give up on dreams. They give up on marriages. They give up on vocations. They give up on others. And they give up on themselves.

There's a high cost to giving up and quitting. There is the suffering of regret over what could have been. There's the loss of ideals, and there are wasted years, ruined potential, and broken promises. Hope keeps you healthy and positive and persevering. It's a light at the end of your tunnel.

An avid football fan spent the afternoon watching his old college team play. All went well in the first half, but then in the third quarter the tide turned against them, and by the middle of the fourth quarter they had fallen far behind. In spite of the fact that his team trailed badly so late in the game, the man never gave up hope. In fact, he was totally confident of victory. What gave him such confidence?

Well, that fan was not worried because he was watching a replay on cable television. He knew from the morning headlines that his team had won. His hope was not based on wishful thinking. It was based on certainty.

It's the same with Christians. God knows the end from the beginning, and he has told us who will win: "I am God, and there is no one like me, declaring the end from the beginning" (Isa 46:9–10).

People with hope are expectant and optimistic and eager. Someone said, "Oh, that's the reason a bird can sing. On the darkest day, he believes in spring." Hope helps us experience an abundant life!

How to Realize Hope

If all of us have such a desperate need for hope, then how can we realize it in our daily lives? We are fortunate as Christians because the scriptures give us many promises concerning hope.

The psalmist said, "Let your steadfast love, O LORD, be upon us, even as we hope in you" (Ps 33:22).

Solomon said, "The hope of the righteous ends in gladness, but the expectation of the wicked comes to nothing.... Hope deferred makes the heart sick" (Prov 10:28; 13:12).

Paul said, "May the God of hope fill you with all joy and peace in believing, so that you may abound in hope by the power of the Holy Spirit" (Rom 15:13).

The writer of Hebrews said, "Christ…was faithful over God's house as a son, and we are his house if we hold firm the confidence and the pride that belong to hope…. When God desired to show even more clearly to the heirs of the promise the unchangeable character of his purpose, he guaranteed it by an oath, so that through two unchangeable things, in which it is impossible that God would prove false, we who have taken refuge might be strongly encouraged to seize the hope set before us. We have this hope, a sure and steadfast anchor of the soul" (Heb 3:6; 6:17–19).

Promises for the future are written in nature. Primitive people saw the beetle emerge from his filthy bed, so they hung up the golden scarab as the symbol of life. They saw the butterfly emerge in glory from her dark cocoon and carved the butterfly as a symbol of the resurrection. Then, seeing the ice and snow melt, and spring convert a cold, dead earth into newness of life, they began to believe in heaven. Every time the sun shines after the storm, hope is born anew. Human beings can't live in despair.

In the fifteenth century in Europe, the whole continent was filled with despair. It was probably the most discouraged time in European history. In 1492, in the Nuremberg Chronicle, a German wrote that the end had come. There was nothing left worth living for. The next year, 1493, a young sailor returned to his Spanish port with the most exciting story. In the midst of this negative environment, Christopher Columbus had discovered a new world.

Hope is alive!

A famous painting shows the devil playing chess with a young man. The devil has just made his move, and the young man's queen is checkmated. On his face is written defeat. One day, a great chess master stood looking at the painting. He carefully studied the positions on the board. Suddenly, his face lighted, and he shouted to the young man in the painting, "You still have a move, son! Don't give up! You still have a move!"

We come to those moments when it seems we are utterly checkmated. Then the great Master of Life comes to us and says, "You still have a move! Don't give up! You still have a move!"

The salvation of the thief on the cross gives us hope. God also gives a wonderful promise of expectation: "He will wipe every tear from their eyes. Death will be no more; mourning and crying and pain will be no more, for the first things have passed away" (Rev 21:4).

How can we realize this wonderful gift from God? How can we feel hopeful and then pass on that gift to others?

To do this we must believe that Jesus offers us not only life, but abundant life! And abundant life includes hope.

       Life More Abundant

Part 2:

The Effects of Abundant Life

A missionary to a primitive culture was speaking when a man asked, "How do you tell those people they need to be saved from their sins?" The missionary replied, "We never try to break down doors. Instead, we wait for a door to open. Our church has about fifty members now, and when someone sees a difference in us and inquires about it, that's an open door."

Then he continued, "Some Americans tell us they witness by handing complete strangers a piece of paper that explains the gospel and then walking away. But it's not that easy here. Unless your life is different enough to open the door, you must keep your mouth shut. In fact, when the first missionary came to our country, he was not trusted. So he didn't preach. He just bought some land, built a home, and began to farm. It took almost two years for someone to ask him why he was different. He led that man to Christ, and the church began."

The questioner was still puzzled and asked, "But what differences would the people of the village see in you and your members?"

The missionary said, "We are honest in our trade. We don't use drugs or alcohol. Fathers don't beat their wives or children. Our young people are respectful. We don't get angry and shun our neighbors. We share our time and possessions without expectation of return. In our little corner of the world, we've learned a very important spiritual principal: We've learned that the one indisputable argument against doubters is a Christlike person."

Jesus said, "You are the light of the world. A city built on a hill cannot be hid…. In the same way, let your light shine before others, so that they may see your good works and give glory to your Father in heaven" (Matt 5:14, 16).

What difference does your faith make in your daily life? A salvation experience brings several gifts of grace. As a new Christian you now have acceptance, love, and value. You have security, forgiveness, and guidance. You have support, purpose, and hope.

These aren't just idle words. They aren't just abstract doctrines. Instead, they are absolute necessities that fill vital human needs. Having our deep needs filled should cause some very real changes to occur in our attitudes and actions.

Are you actually benefitting from these gifts? Are they fulfilling you? Furthermore, are you passing these benefits on to others?

Paul says, "Blessed be the God and Father of our Lord Jesus Christ, the Father of mercies and the God of all consolation, who consoles us in all our affliction, so that we may be able to console those who are in any affliction with the consolation with which we ourselves are consoled by God" (2 Cor 1:3–4).

Are you letting your faith affect your life and your relationships in a positive way? For instance, if you're married, are you a better spouse because you're a Christian? Paul said, "The husband should give to his wife her conjugal rights, and likewise the wife to her husband" (1 Cor 7:3). Furthermore, in a day when marriages were not always based on love, he said, "Husbands, love your wives" (Eph 5:25).

Paul was also practical. He said, "And whoever does not provide for relatives, and especially for family members, has denied the faith and is worse than an unbeliever" (1 Tim 5:8).

Physical needs must be filled. This includes being industrious and bringing home a paycheck. So as Christian husbands and wives you will care for each other. You will show respect for each other, and you will reflect the love God has shown you in your behavior toward your mate.

If you have children, are you a better parent because you are a Christian? Solomon said, "The righteous walk in integrity—happy are the children who follow them!... Train children in the right way, and when old, they will not stray" (Prov 20:7; 22:6). Paul said, "Fathers, do not provoke your children to anger, but bring them up in the discipline and instruction of the Lord" (Eph 6:4). As Christian parents you will be moral examples and role models. You will bring your children to church for Bible study and worship. Your discipline will be consistent but fair. You will never shame or demean your children.

If you have a job, are you a better employee because you are a Christian? The writer of Ecclesiastes said, "Whatever your hand finds to do, do with your might" (Eccl 9:10). Paul said, "Do not lag in zeal, be ardent in spirit, serve the Lord" (Rom 12:11). He also said, "Whatever your task, put yourselves into it, as done for the Lord and not for your masters" (Col 3:23). So as Christian employees you must be good workers. You must be diligent and accountable. Remember, as a witness, your actions are more powerful than your words!

If you have acquaintances, are you a better friend and neighbor because you are a Christian? Solomon said, "A friend loves at all times" (Prov 17:17).

Jesus said, "'Do not judge, and you will not be judged; do not condemn, and you will not be condemned. Forgive, and you will be forgiven'" (Luke 6:37). He also said, "By this everyone will know that you are my disciples, if you have love for one another" (John 13:35). So as Christian friends and neighbors you will be helpful, kind, and encouraging. You won't judge, criticize, and gossip. You will overlook slights and extend forgiveness.

If you live in America, are you a better citizen because you are a Christian? The writer of Chronicles said, "If my people who are called by my name humble themselves, pray, seek my face, and turn from their wicked ways, then I will hear from heaven, and will forgive their sin and heal their land" (2 Chron 7:14). Jesus said, "Blessed are the peacemakers, for they will be called children of God" (Matt 5:9). Paul said, "If it is possible, so far as it depends on you, live peaceably with all" (Rom 12:18). He also said, "First of all, then, I urge that supplications, prayers, intercessions, and thanksgivings be made for everyone, for kings and all who are in high positions, so that we may lead a quiet and peaceable life in all godliness and dignity" (1 Tim 2:1–2). So as Christian citizens you will be concerned about your government. You will study issues before you vote. You will express your opinions in an informed and constructive way. You will realize that negative criticism and partisan attacks are not useful. Instead, we are to support and pray for our leaders.

Does your faith make a difference in your family?

Does your faith make a difference in your workplace?

Does your faith make a difference in your neighborhood?

Does your faith make a difference in your nation?

If your faith doesn't affect your whole life and those around you, then your conversion was incomplete. Jesus said, "If you love me, you will keep my commandments" (John 14:15). Paul said, "Show yourself in all respects a model of good works, and in your teaching show integrity, gravity" (Titus 2:7). John said, "Whoever says, 'I abide in him,' ought to walk just as he walked" (1 John 2:6).

So what "gifts of grace" did you receive from God when you were converted? What are the benefits of your faith, and what differences do they make?

1. Feeling accepted abolishes shame. You no longer have to deny your faults and cover up your weaknesses. You don't have to claim self-righteousness and live hypocritically. You don't have to be ashamed, because God accepts you as you are.

2. Feeling loved abolishes hatred. You no longer have to be jealous of smart people or envious of rich people. You don't have to compete for attention and praise. You don't have to hate, because God loves you unconditionally.

3. Feeling valued abolishes worthlessness. You no longer have to boast and brag about your accomplishments. You don't have to compromise your moral standards in order to please people. You don't have to feel worthless, because God gives you great value.

4. Feeling secure abolishes insecurity. You no longer have to be afraid to make a mistake. You don't have to amass wealth or possessions to protect your status. You don't have to feel insecure, because God is with you forever.

5. Feeling forgiven abolishes guilt. You don't have to feel guilty, because God has granted you absolute forgiveness for every sin. You no longer have to criticize and judge others to excuse your own failures. You won't feel a need for revenge to settle scores.

6. Having guidance abolishes confusion. You no longer have to be paralyzed by uncertainty. You don't have to waste time and energy on dead-end streets. You don't have to learn everything by trial and error. You can trust your own instincts and common sense. You don't have to be confused, because God gives wisdom and guidance when we ask.

7. Having support abolishes weakness. You no longer have to hesitate or avoid involvement in life. You don't have to discount your abilities and claim inadequacy. You don't have to experience weakness, because God gives you strength.

8. Having a purpose abolishes aimlessness. You no longer have to live idle, lazy lives. You don't have to operate with a lack of direction and focus. You don't have to be aimless, because God has a special purpose for you, and you can discover it.

9. Having hope abolishes despair. You no longer have to dread the future. You don't have to suffer endless depression. You don't have to experience a sense of pessimism and futility. You don't have to feel despair, because God offers hope.

Salvation is a life change; it's not just a ticket to heaven. As a matter of fact, it's more like a gift certificate to an abundant life.

Listen to these verses: Paul said, "So if anyone is in Christ, there is a new creation: everything old has passed away; see, everything has become new!" (2 Cor 5:17); "I have been crucified with Christ; and it is no longer I who live, but it is Christ who lives in me" (Gal 2:19–20); "You were taught to put away your former way of life, your old self, corrupt and deluded by its lusts, and to be renewed in the spirit of your minds, and to clothe yourselves with the new self, created according to the likeness of God in true righteousness and holiness" (Eph 4:22–24); "[You] have clothed yourselves with the new self, which is being renewed in knowledge according to the image of its creator" (Col 3:10).

As Christians, God has given us this wonderful new life. But we must take advantage of its benefits. We must let the fruit of the Spirit make a permanent difference in our attitudes and behavior. We must let the God within give us joy, peace, and confidence, and then we must pass these benefits on to others.

Acceptance

A salvation experience makes a tangible difference in a person's life. It makes a difference because it fills basic human needs, and when these needs are filled, negative urges and reactions are abolished. For instance, when we're rejected, the shame we feel causes us to react in destructive ways. But when we realize that God accepts us just as we are, these problems are eliminated. This change is called conversion.

God knows we yearn for acceptance. Jesus said, "Your Father knows what you need before you ask him" (Matt 6:8), and Jesus knew what it was like to be rejected.

He was also perceptive. Scripture says, "Jesus…would not entrust himself to them, because he knew all people and needed no one to testify about anyone; for he himself knew what was in everyone" (John 2:24–25). This means he understood the deep psychological needs and problems of human beings.

The Need for Acceptance

We are born with survival instincts that tend to make us selfish and defensive. Furthermore, we all grow up in imperfect environments. Even the best parents make mistakes and cause feelings of inadequacy. As fathers and mothers try to keep their children safe and instill morality, they invariably say and do things that make these children feel insufficient. When boys and girls hear "No!" over and over, they begin to experience feelings of self-doubt. Children don't understand the overall meaning of things. They take every word and action literally and personally.

For instance, one well-educated, successful man spoke of his childhood: "For years I felt inadequate. When I was five years old, I went to school with my nine-year-old brother, Jim. Every morning my mom would say, 'I'm giving your lunch money to Jim, because you might lose it.' I didn't know she did that because he was four years older. I thought it was because I was not responsible. For many years these feelings of inadequacy hampered my decisions and sabotaged my successes."

We are constantly pressured to measure up, even by our loved ones. For instance, if a neighbor spilled a glass of milk, you'd say, "Oh, don't worry about it." But if your child did the exact same thing, you'd probably yell and maybe punish him.

Most of us overlook the "innocent" little quirks of a friend, but we criticize and nag about those same quirks in our spouse's behavior.

Some of us feel rejection because of our gender. If my parents wanted a boy and I'm a girl, then I'm not right.

Some of us feel rejection because of our race or nationality. If I'm different from most of my neighbors, then I'm not right.

Some of us feel rejection because of our personality. If I don't think and feel and act just like the rest of my family, then I'm not right.

Over the years, when we were the last one chosen for a spelling bee, we felt rejected. When we didn't make the cheerleading squad, we felt rejected. When we were fired from a job or faced a divorce, we felt rejected. Life does a number on everyone. Feeling rejected is a universal problem, and feeling accepted is a universal need.

Negative Effects of Rejection

Rejection hurts so much that most of us try desperately to gain acceptance. To do this we deny our faults and hide our flaws. We cover our errors and blame others for our failures. We attempt to live up to authority figures' standards. This takes a lot of energy and puts stress on our bodies.

In some cases we seek acceptance by appearing overly pious. We use religious phrases, denounce sinful acts, and give the impression that we are "holier than thou." We become self-righteous and legalistic like the Pharisees and moral fanatics.

Living this way turns us into hypocrites, which means we have to wear masks and armor. We have to pretend and play roles. In the process we lose our God-given, authentic personality and begin to live a lie.

All of these undesirable actions are vain attempts to gain the acceptance we need.

How Does God Fill Our Need for Acceptance?

In one Bible story Jesus offered an immoral Samaritan woman this acceptance, and she became a missionary. This illustrates how salvation can make a real, tangible difference in a life. John said,

> A Samaritan woman came to draw water, and Jesus said to her, "Give me a drink." (His disciples had gone to the city to buy food.) The Samaritan woman said to him, "How is

it that you, a Jew, ask a drink of me, a woman of Samaria?"
(Jews do not share things in common with Samaritans.) Jesus
answered her, "If you knew the gift of God, and who it is that
is saying to you, 'Give me a drink,' you would have asked
him, and he would have given you living water." The woman
said to him, "Sir, you have no bucket, and the well is deep.
Where do you get that living water? Are you greater than our
ancestor Jacob, who gave us the well, and with his sons and
his flocks drank from it?" Jesus said to her, "Everyone who
drinks of this water will be thirsty again, but those who drink
of the water that I will give them will never be thirsty. The
water that I will give will become in them a spring of water
gushing up to eternal life." The woman said to him, "Sir, give
me this water, so that I may never be thirsty or have to keep
coming here to draw water."

Jesus said to her, "Go, call your husband, and come
back." The woman answered him, "I have no husband." Jesus
said to her, "You are right in saying, 'I have no husband'; for
you have had five husbands, and the one you have now is
not your husband. What you have said is true!" The woman
said to him, "Sir, I see that you are a prophet. Our ancestors worshiped on this mountain, but you say that the place
where people must worship is in Jerusalem." Jesus said to
her, "Woman, believe me, the hour is coming when you will
worship the Father neither on this mountain nor in Jerusalem. You worship what you do not know; we worship what we
know, for salvation is from the Jews. But the hour is coming,
and is now here, when the true worshipers will worship the
Father in spirit and truth, for the Father seeks such as these
to worship him. God is spirit, and those who worship him
must worship in spirit and truth." The woman said to him, "I
know that Messiah is coming" (who is called Christ). "When
he comes, he will proclaim all things to us." Jesus said to her,
"I am he, the one who is speaking to you."

Just then his disciples came. They were astonished that
he was speaking with a woman, but no one said, "What
do you want?" or, "Why are you speaking with her?" Then

the woman left her water jar and went back to the city.
(John 4:7–28)

This woman had been rejected by her peers. Samaritans were considered to be second-class citizens. Most Jews shunned and ridiculed them. Therefore, the woman was living with shame. She avoided coming to the community well in the evening and instead came in the heat of the day. That's how she met Jesus.

Notice that all these years of being rejected and demeaned had not helped her in any way. It had not changed her or caused her to repent. Rather, it had forced her into a most unproductive lifestyle: with five husbands and now a live-in lover.

Rejection never accomplishes redemption. It never causes people to improve. It never corrects their faults. Instead, it causes problems as we try to defend ourselves and gain acceptance.

Our false beliefs about ourselves and God create feelings of rejection that lead to shame. The psalmist prayed, "Do not hide your face from your servant, for I am in distress—make haste to answer me.... You know the insults I receive, and my shame and dishonor; my foes are all known to you" (Ps 69:17, 19).

Since God knows our human condition, he created a plan to rectify the situation. The Samaritan woman is an example of this miracle. She had many of these negative characteristics because she had been rejected. Religious people felt they had a legal right to condemn and reject her. In fact, by human standards, she probably deserved scorn and criticism, but Jesus didn't berate her for promiscuity. He didn't demand that she confess and repent. He didn't require her to quit "living in sin." Instead, he accepted her just as she was. He knew that such acceptance would enable her to recognize her problems and overcome her weaknesses. He showed this acceptance by speaking to her, which was not allowed in Jewish society. He also asked for a favor, which gave her status and showed that he considered her as an equal. Furthermore, he answered her theological questions, assuring her that she was not inferior because she was a woman or a Samaritan. Then he offered her the gift of "living water." This changed her life.

Has Jesus's acceptance of you changed your life? If you really believe Jesus's wonderful promise about acceptance, it will change your life. He said,

"Everything that the Father gives me will come to me, and anyone who comes to me I will never drive away" (John 6:37).

This invitation includes sinners of every description. No one is too damaged or too wicked or too late. An updated version of the parable of the prodigal son may explain this unbelievable gift of grace: A teenager got mad at her parents and ran away from home. Her family searched for her, but she dropped out of sight in the drug and prostitution culture of the 1960s. Hungry, dirty, sick, and desperate, she came home and knocked on the door. When her grieving father saw her, do you think he said, "Oh, is that you at last? Well, it's too late. You've messed up once too often. Just go back to the streets!"? Or did he say, "You're a sight. If you'll go clean up and take something for that cough, we might let you in!"?

Of course, he didn't do that! That father opened his arms and his heart and joyfully took her in, *just as she was*! That's acceptance! That's how God accepts us!

All of us have troubled pasts. All of us have made mistakes. All of us have deep needs that must be filled. But there is a solution to our problems. Paul said, "My God will fully satisfy every need of yours" (Phil 4:19).

If you come to Christ, you will never be rejected. You will have no reason to be ashamed. You will not need to deny your faults and hide your flaws. You will not need to claim self-righteousness and pretend to be "holier than thou." You will not need to be a hypocrite. This change will make you happier, and it will improve your relationship with others. A Christian conversion will make you a better mate, parent, friend, neighbor, and citizen because you won't be reacting in destructive ways to gain acceptance.

The salvation story is designed to turn rejection into acceptance. If you come to Christ, you are accepted just as you are. That's the gospel. And that's why the salvation experience makes a difference in your life.

Love

A salvation experience makes a tangible difference in a person's life. It makes a difference because it fills basic human needs, and when these needs are filled, negative urges and reactions are abolished. For instance, when we are *unloved*, the emptiness and anger we feel cause us to react in destructive ways. But when we realize that God loves us unconditionally, these problems are eliminated. This change is called conversion.

God knows we yearn for unconditional love. Jesus said, "Your Father knows what you need before you ask him" (Matt 6:8). Jesus knew what it was like to be unloved. Isaiah said, "He was despised and rejected by others; a man of suffering and acquainted with infirmity" (Isa 53:3).

He was also perceptive. Scripture says, "Jesus…needed no one to testify about anyone; for he himself knew what was in everyone" (John 2:24–25). This means he understood the deep psychological needs and problems of human beings.

The Need for Love

We are born with survival instincts that tend to make us selfish and egocentric. Furthermore, we all grow up in imperfect environments. Even the best parents fail to show total love. Since parents are also human, they have their own issues and blind spots. In dealing with their personal needs, they invariably say and do things that make children feel unloved. When moms and dads promise "I'll love you if you eat your cereal" or someone threatens "Daddy won't love you if you break his tools," children assume love is a reward that is only given as a result of good behavior.

Once, when a teacher asked her students to write down three wishes, several expressed their desperate need for love. One said, "I wish I could get straight A's so my dad would love me." Another said, "I wish everyone in my family loved each other."

Also, small children do not understand reasons for actions. When an older child sees a baby being cuddled and held, he thinks it is loved more than he is, and sibling rivalry develops. If a sick or handicapped child gets a lot of time and attention, his sisters and brothers may view that as more love.

Furthermore, children often measure love by time, and unfortunately most parents today are short of that. When you spend more time at work, watching TV, or attending meetings than you do with them, boys and girls interpret that to mean "You care more for those things than you do for me."

In fact, most of the "love" of our friends and even family members is based on an *if* or *because* kind of love:

If love says, "I'll love you . . .

    If you let me borrow your car;

    If you wear the right kind of clothes;

    If you do what I tell you to do;

    If you loan me money when I ask;

    If you agree with me about everything."

Because love says, "I love you . . .

    Because you are an excellent athlete;

    Because you supported me when I ran for office;

    Because you are popular and friendly;

    Because you are pretty;

    Because you are basically a lot like me."

These offerings are not love. They are deals or trades. Furthermore, they are temporary. When circumstances change or when we fall short of expectations, the "love" disappears.

Unconditional love is rare. That's because it's hard for individuals who don't feel unconditional love themselves to give unconditional love to others. Therefore, almost all of us reach adulthood starved for love. Few of us remember the names of those famous people who won Oscars or Heisman Trophies or Nobel Peace Prizes. We've forgotten most vice presidents and war heroes. We can't recall the names of popular cheerleaders in high school or maybe even that person we had a crush on.

But there is one thing none of us ever forget, and that's a person who really loved us. Think about it. Who in your life gave you that precious gift of real love with no strings attached? Was it a parent, a grandparent, a brother or sister, an aunt or uncle, a teacher, a coach, a neighbor, an employee, or a pastor?

Throughout his ministry Jesus emphasized love. He told his disciples over and over again that God loves them, but they didn't believe him. So he showed them by dying on the cross.

Effects of a Lack of Love

Feeling unloved hurts so much that most of us try desperately to gain love. We may try to earn it by doing favors or by resorting to flattery. We may compromise our moral principles in order to get attention and approval. Promiscuity often results when we try to substitute sex for love. Anger is a common result of the lack of love, and it's expressed in the forms of jealousy, envy, and animosity toward others. In some cases we become overly competitive. Every encounter becomes a contest. Every activity becomes a battle. Every associate becomes an adversary.

We must win every argument. We must attack any opposition. We manipulate situations to get praise and rewards. This behavior finally alienates us from other people. Without friends and supporters, our lives become bleak and full of hatred and bitterness.

All of these undesirable actions are vain attempts to gain the love we need.

How Does God Fill Our Need for Love?

In one Bible story Jesus extends unconditional love to a deceitful, greedy man named Zacchaeus, and his attitude and behavior were drastically altered from that day forward. This illustrates how salvation can make a real, tangible difference in our lives. Luke says,

> [Jesus] entered Jericho and was passing through it. A man was there named Zacchaeus; he was a chief tax collector and was rich. He was trying to see who Jesus was, but on account of the crowd he could not, because he was short in stature. So he ran ahead and climbed a sycamore tree to see him, because he was going to pass that way. When Jesus came to the place, he looked up and said to him, "Zacchaeus, hurry and come down; for I must stay at your house today." So he hurried down and was happy to welcome him. All who saw it began to grumble and said, "He has gone to be the guest of one who is a sinner." Zacchaeus stood there and said to the Lord, "Look, half of my possessions, Lord, I will give to the poor; and if I have defrauded anyone of anything, I will pay back four times as much." Then Jesus said to him, "Today salvation has come to this house, because he too is a son of Abraham. For the Son of Man came to seek out and to save the lost." (Luke 19:1–10)

This man had been hated and despised. He didn't have friends and neighbors who cared about him. Neither his fellow citizens nor his enemies showed any affection for him. He was "a man without a country." He fraternized with the occupying forces. His career and lifestyle were disgraceful. He cheated his own countrymen for personal gain. In other words, he was not a very nice man!

He wouldn't have been named "citizen of the year." He couldn't have been elected mayor of Jericho. Everyone resents such traitors. In addition, his small size probably caused even more disrespect and rudeness. Therefore, Zacchaeus became more and more alienated and hostile.

Notice that all the hatred and condemnation Zacchaeus received had not helped him in any way. It had not caused him to be patriotic or benevolent. Rather, he had become more antisocial and covetous. Hostility never accomplishes redemption. It never causes people to improve. It never corrects their faults. Instead, it causes problems as we try to defend ourselves and gain unconditional love. Our false beliefs about ourselves and God create feelings of anger that lead to hatred. Paul described this condition so well: "For we ourselves were once foolish, disobedient, led astray, slaves to various passions and pleasures, passing our days in malice and envy, despicable, hating one another. But when the goodness and loving kindness of God our Savior appeared, he saved us, not because of any works of righteousness that we had done, but according to his mercy, through the water of rebirth and renewal by the Holy Spirit" (Titus 3:3–5).

Since God knows our human condition, he created a plan to rectify the situation. Zacchaeus is an example of this miracle. He had many of these negative characteristics because of a lack of love. We can understand why people would resent and shun a greedy traitor, but Jesus didn't do that. He didn't point fingers at him. He didn't say, "You're unpatriotic." He didn't lecture him on cheating. Instead, he extended warmth and love. He knew that would enable him to solve all his other problems.

Jesus extended love to Zacchaeus by noticing him and calling him by name. He demonstrated his personal concern by associating with him. He actually went to his home and shared a meal with him. To Jews this meant that he was treating him as an affectionate equal, and it changed his life.

Has Jesus's love for you changed your life? If you really believe Jesus's wonderful promise about love, it will change your life. He said, "This is my commandment, that you love one another as I have loved you. No one has greater love than this, to lay down one's life for one's friends" (John 15:12–13).

This love, which caused him to give his life, is offered to sinners of every description. No one is too unlovable or too offensive or too disagreeable. God doesn't love us if we're good or because we're moral. Rather, it's his love that enables us to be good and moral. John said, "We love because he first loved us" (1 John 4:19).

Long ago, a young man disobeyed his parents, abused his siblings, and left home. His father promised, "Son, we'll put a light in the window until you return."

Over the years they heard of his drunken brawls, but the light still burned. They heard of his crimes, but the light still burned. They heard of his addiction to drugs, but the light still burned. No matter what the wayward son did, his parents' love never dimmed. The light still burned!

God's love is like that. It's everlasting. He loved us before we loved him. He loves us while we are in sin. He loves us through our problems and weaknesses and failures. The light still burns! He loves us unconditionally.

All of us have troubled pasts. All of us have made mistakes. All of us have deep needs that must be filled. But there is a solution to our problems. Paul said, "My God will fully satisfy every need of yours" (Phil 4:19).

If you come to Christ, you will never be unloved. You will have no reason to be jealous or envious. You will not have to fight for attention and praise.

This change will make you happier and it will improve your relationship with others. A Christian conversion will make you a better mate, parent, friend, neighbor, and citizen because you won't be reacting in destructive ways to gain love.

The salvation story is designed to turn hatred into love. If you come to Christ, you will discover that you are loved unconditionally. That's the gospel, and that's why the salvation experience makes a difference in your life!

Value

A salvation experience makes a tangible difference in a person's life. It makes a difference because it fills basic human needs, and when these needs are filled, negative urges and reactions are abolished. For instance, when we are treated as worthless, the discouragement we feel causes us to react in destructive ways. But when we realize that God values us, these problems are eliminated. This change is called conversion.

God knows we yearn for self-worth and value. Jesus said, "Your Father knows what you need before you ask him" (Matt 6:8). Jesus had personal experience with this problem. Isaiah said, "He was despised, and we held him of no account" (Isa 53:3).

He was also perceptive. Scripture says, "Jesus…needed no one to testify about anyone; for he himself knew what was in everyone" (John 2:24–25). This means he understood the deep psychological needs and problems of human beings.

The Need for a Sense of Value

We are born with a lot of potential but few abilities. As babies we can't really achieve very much on our own. Furthermore, we all grow up in imperfect environments. As children we must obey other people. Adults and authority figures make our decisions and dictate our lives. Our opinions are disregarded. We're taught to deprecate ourselves and our accomplishments. We are told that we're bad over and over again.

Once, a little boy and his sister were arguing and their mom yelled, "Why can't you two ever get along and play nice?"

"Oh, Mommy," the little girl replied, "we do that lots of times, but then you don't notice."

In the home, at school, and in public, kids are neglected and ignored. They interpret that to mean "we're not very important." One mother hired a new babysitter, and her child heard her say, "I shouldn't leave my jewelry laying around. I don't know if I can trust this girl." The child thought, "Well, my mother trusts her to take care of me, so I must not be as valuable as her jewelry."

When we are criticized or ridiculed, we feel worthless. When we miss math problems on a test, we feel worthless. When others shame and bully us, we feel worthless. When we don't know answers to questions, we feel worthless. When our projects are unsuccessful, we feel worthless. When we fail at an interview, we feel worthless. When we don't get that job we wanted, we feel worthless. Teachers check what's wrong with big red marks but seldom mention what's right. Since we learn by trial and error, we have many failures. Then we think that because we experience failures that we are a failure.

Also, children don't understand situations and often misinterpret the reason for things. For instance, children who are adopted often feel that they were given away because they were worthless. Children who are abused feel they are being hurt because they deserve it. Children who are abandoned or neglected believe it's their fault. A therapist said, "It's a law of life that if you disown a child, then when they're older, they will disown themselves."

As adults we recall every dumb thing we ever did. We remember our mistakes and our embarrassing blunders. We compare ourselves to others who seem to have more money, more success, or more recognition than we have. We overrate the rich and famous. Advertisers and soap operas insinuate that unless we are a fabulous musician or actor or artist, we are not important.

Self-worth is fragile. Real self-worth includes self-respect.

Effects of Lacking a Sense of Value

A sense of worthlessness hurts so much that most of us try desperately to achieve value. To do this we may strive for perfection. We may cling more closely to our own moral systems and extol our own standards and beliefs. We may be prejudiced against minorities because we need someone worse off than us to look down on. We may judge and put down others in order to make ourselves look better. We may identify with famous people to gain significance. We may try to appease our critics by pretending to agree. We may compromise our convictions in order to be accepted. We may attempt to live out the demands of parents and give up our own dreams. We may overreact by becoming workaholics, vainly attempting to justify our misguided self-evaluation.

People without self-worth may punish themselves by getting into destructive relationships and allowing abuse. Since they don't feel they deserve success, they often sabotage their projects.

All of these undesirable actions are vain attempts to gain the self-worth we need.

How Does God Fill Our Need for a Sense of Value?

In one Bible story, Jesus affirmed the value of a Roman military officer, who became a believer and had his prayers answered. This illustrates how salvation can make a tangible difference in a life. Matthew says,

> When [Jesus] entered Capernaum, a centurion came to him, appealing to him and saying, "Lord, my servant is lying at home paralyzed, in terrible distress." And he said to him, "I will come and cure him." The centurion answered, "Lord, I am not worthy to have you come under my roof; but only speak the word, and my servant will be healed. For I also am a man under authority, with soldiers under me; and I say to one, 'Go,' and he goes, and to another, 'Come,' and he comes, and to my slave, 'Do this,' and the slave does it." When Jesus heard him, he was amazed and said to those who followed him, "Truly I tell you, in no one in Israel have I found such faith…. And to the centurion Jesus said, "Go; let it be done for you according to your faith." And the servant was healed in that hour." (Matt 8:5–10, 13)

This army officer was not in a position or location to have his religion validated or honored. He was an alien and looked down upon as an atheist. This Roman was an enemy of the Jews. His army was occupying their land and enslaving the population. The Pharisees and publicans considered all Romans as infidels and sinners. They were not "God's chosen ones"; thus, their religion was worthless. They were not allowed in the temple for worship and would not have been welcomed in the synagogues or invited to fellowship with Jews. Even so, out of his human compassion for a mere servant, this centurion dared approach Jesus. Instead of pulling rank or demanding attention, he was willing to relate to Jesus in any way possible. He assumed, because he wasn't a Jew, that the Lord would not consider going into his house.

Yet he dared to ask him for help. He may have expected a refusal or at least a reprimand for his lack of orthodox faith. Instead, Jesus immediately responded with praise. Even though the Roman's spiritual state is unknown, he certainly was not an overt follower of Jesus. He represents the secular person who isn't a traditional Christian. He represents those of our associates who may be from non-Christian backgrounds. Religious people are often disdainful of such individuals, but Jesus was not.

Notice that all these years of being ostracized and judged had not helped this soldier in any way. It had not changed him or caused him to become an orthodox worshiper. Rather, it had forced him to live apart from the Hebrew faith as an outsider.

Failing to esteem and respect those who are different never accomplishes redemption. It never causes people to improve. It never corrects their faults. Instead, it causes problems as we try to defend ourselves and gain value.

Our false beliefs about ourselves and God create feelings of worthlessness that lead to discouragement. The psalmist expressed his feelings this way: "I am a worm, and not human; scorned by others, and despised by the people. All who see me mock at me; they make mouths at me, they shake their heads" (Ps 22:6–7).

Since God knows our human condition, he created a plan to rectify the situation. The Roman Centurion is an example of this miracle. It's obvious that most of the people who interacted with that soldier were suspicious and critical. Few people like military leaders with the take-charge personality this man had. And, of course, it's natural to be antagonistic to those in opposition to our culture and religion. But Jesus was open and tolerant. He didn't try to convert him or point out the errors of his religion. Instead, he listened to his request and immediately offered to go home with him. This showed that he valued him and his spiritual concern. He even complimented and affirmed his faith, and this changed his life and answered his prayer.

Has Jesus's esteem for you changed your life? If you really believe Jesus's wonderful promise about your value, it will change your life. He said, "Do not be afraid; you are of more value than many sparrows" (Matt 10:31). This value includes sinners of every description. No one is too insignificant or too poor or too uneducated.

A young boy had a terrible childhood. He was abused and abandoned. Furthermore, he had a learning disability that caused him to be ridiculed and punished in school. No one had ever helped him to discover any strengths or talents until a coach saw his athletic ability and spent time and effort developing it.

The young man got a basketball scholarship to college, but still none of this really improved his self-esteem until finally a scout saw him play and offered him a lucrative professional contract. Then, all at once, he thought, "Hey, maybe I'm worth something. I must be more valuable than I thought. These people are willing to pay a high price for me." That's exactly what God did. Paul said, "You were bought with a price; do not become slaves of human masters" (1 Cor 7:23).

All of us have troubled pasts. All of us have regrets and remorse. All of us have made mistakes. All of us have deep needs that must be filled. But there is an answer to our questions. There is a solution to our problems. Paul said, "My God will fully satisfy every need of yours" (Phil 4:19).

If you come to Christ, you will never be worthless. You will have no reason to feel discouraged. You will not need to boast or brag. You won't have to compromise your convictions to get others' approval. You won't have to be a workaholic in order to prove your worth.

This change will make you happier, and it will improve your relationship with others. A Christian conversion will make you a better mate, parent, friend, neighbor, employee, and citizen because you won't be reacting in destructive ways in order to gain significance and prove your worth.

The salvation story is designed to turn worthlessness into great value. If you come to Christ, you are valued just as you are. That's the gospel, and that's why the salvation experience makes a difference in your life.

Security

A salvation experience makes a tangible difference in a person's life. It makes a difference because it fills basic human needs, and when these needs are filled, negative urges and reactions are abolished.   For instance, when we are insecure, the anxiety we feel causes us to react in destructive ways. But when we realize that God gives us total security, these problems are eliminated. This change is called conversion.

God knows we yearn for security. Jesus said, "Your Father knows what you need before you ask him" (Matt 6:8). Jesus knew what it was like to feel insecure and depressed. Scripture says, "He took with him Peter and the two sons of Zebedee, and began to be grieved and agitated. Then he said to them, 'I am deeply grieved, even to death; remain here, and stay awake with me'" (Matt 26:37–38).

He was also perceptive. Scripture says, "Jesus…needed no one to testify about anyone; for he himself knew what was in everyone" (John 2:24–25). This means he understood the deep psychological needs and problems of human beings.

The Need for Security

We are born with survival instincts of self-preservation that tend to make us fearful and anxious. Furthermore, we all grow up in imperfect environments.

Feeling safe is essential for children. All boys and girls need shelter and protection. Living with stress is damaging to our health. Babies who are neglected or abandoned have issues with security. Those who grow up with abuse and violence either in their homes or communities pay a price with physical and emotional problems. Existing in a state of fight/flight takes its toll on our bodies and spirits.

All of us need consistency and stability, and all of us have trust issues. Life is hard, and the future is unknown. All of us have had people let us down. All of us have had loved ones die. All of us have had friends move away. All of us have had relationships disintegrate. Bad things happen, even to good people! As much as we'd like to control the conditions and events around us, we know we can't! Earthquakes and tornadoes, floods and fires are examples of natural catastrophes. Terrorist attacks and wars are inevitable. Accidents occur. Jobs are lost. Every time we turn on the TV, we see examples of horrendous crimes.

Drugs and gangs are epidemic. Burglaries and home invasions are all too common. Most news stories are of violence.

Everyone has felt like the poet who said, "O God, this ocean is so large, and my boat is so small." At times we feel at the mercy of the elements. It seems there is a tragedy or a crisis around every corner. There are diseases looming ahead for us and for our families. Too often, religion adds to our fears with threats of God's wrath and damnation. And then there is the final, inevitable enemy—death!

Effects of Insecurity

Being insecure hurts so much that most of us try desperately to achieve a sense of security. To do this we may become obsessed with obedience. We may be legalistic and compulsive. By trying to keep every rule and regulation perfectly, we leave no room for normal human error. We may let "keeping the letter of the Law" override compassion and common sense. That's why the Pharisees criticized Jesus for healing on the Sabbath. Fear and lack of assurance make us so cautious that we can't operate. We can't explore. We can't try new things. We can't risk. We become like the little man with the one talent. We hide our light and avoid involvement. Insecurity may lead to greed as we try to amass enough wealth or possessions to protect us against the dangers of poverty and homelessness.

All of these undesirable actions are vain attempts to gain the security we need.

How Does God Fill Our Need for Security?

In one Bible story Jesus promises security to a Jewish religious leader named Nicodemus. After his encounter with Jesus, he was willing to identify himself as a follower, even though that was not a popular thing to do. This illustrates how salvation can make a tangible difference in a life. John says,

> Now there was a Pharisee named Nicodemus, a leader of the Jews. He came to Jesus by night and said to him, "Rabbi, we know that you are a teacher who has come from God; for no one can do these signs that you do apart from the presence of God." Jesus answered him, "Very truly, I tell you, no one can see the kingdom of God without being born from above.... Very truly, I tell you, we speak of what we know and testify to what we have seen; yet you do not receive our testimony.... And just as Moses lifted up the serpent in the wilderness, so

must the Son of Man be lifted up, that whoever believes in him may have eternal life. For God so loved the world that he gave his only Son, so that everyone who believes in him may not perish but may have eternal life. Indeed, God did not send the Son into the world to condemn the world, but in order that the world might be saved through him. Those who believe in him are not condemned; but those who do not believe are condemned already, because they have not believed in the name of the only Son of God. (John 3:1–3, 11, 14–18)

Later, Nicodemus gave evidence of his faith by assisting at the Lord's burial. The scriptures say, "Nicodemus, who had at first come to Jesus by night, also came, bringing a mixture of myrrh and aloes, weighing about a hundred pounds. They took the body of Jesus and wrapped it with the spices in linen cloths, according to the burial custom of the Jews" (John 19:39–40).

As a member of the Sanhedrin and a religious authority, Nicodemus had lived by rules and regulations. These Pharisees were devout individuals, yet they were still insecure. They still lived in constant fear that they might break a law or anger God and be punished. Therefore, they became fanatical and legalistic. But Nicodemus was an honest seeker. He knew this wasn't enough.

The fact that he asked theological questions shows that he was unsure about his spiritual state. Notice that all these years of being cautious and law-abiding and fearful had not helped him in any way. Studying theology and teaching morals had not fulfilled Nicodemus. It had not changed him or given him peace. Rather, it had forced him into a most unproductive and unpleasant lifestyle. We know he was extremely well educated and highly respected in legal circles, but his need was great.

Legalism and obedience out of fear never accomplishes redemption. It never causes people to improve. It never corrects their faults. Instead, it causes problems as we try to defend ourselves and gain security.

Our false beliefs about ourselves and God create feelings of insecurity that lead to anxiety. Such fears are not valid. Scripture says, "I am convinced that neither death, nor life, nor angels, nor rulers, nor things present, nor things to come, nor powers, nor height, nor depth, nor anything else in all creation, will be able to separate us from the love of God in Christ Jesus our Lord" (Rom 8:38–39).

Since God knows our human condition, he created a plan to rectify the situation. Nicodemus is an example of this miracle. He showed evidence of an insecure and fearful personality. He didn't meet Jesus in an open forum. Instead, he came alone. Also, the fact that he approached Jesus by night shows his insecurity. Neither his background, his education, his status in society, his position on the court, nor his moral lifestyle gave him peace and assurance. But Jesus met his need by explaining God's promise of his eternal presence and protection and eternal life. This promise is not to particular groups of people or types of people. It is to the whole world. Furthermore, this promise is not based on our actions or behavior. It is a gift of grace.

Has Jesus's assurance of security changed your life? If you really believe Jesus's wonderful promise about security, it will change your life. He said, "Very truly, I tell you, whoever believes has eternal life" (John 6:47).

This promise is to sinners of every description. No one is too damaged or too wicked or too late. The story about a mother and her naughty little boy illustrates this principle. It seems the child was incorrigible. He had broken every rule and disobeyed every command. He had driven his poor mom crazy all day. He yelled, "I hate you! And I don't have to mind you." Finally, she sent him to his room and went out into the garden. Suddenly, someone shouted, "Ma'am, your house is on fire!" She looked up and saw the smoke and flames from a second-story window.

Now, did this mother say, "Well, he's probably set his room on fire deliberately. He deserves to suffer the consequences. I'll just let him die"? Of course she didn't. You know what she did: She dashed into that house and risked her very life to save her child before doing anything else. God is like that, "not wanting any to perish" (see 2 Pet 3:9).

All of us have troubled pasts. All of us have doubts and dreads and worries. All of us have fears and insecurities. All of us have deep needs that must be filled. But there are answers to our questions. There are solutions to our problems. Paul said, "My God will fully satisfy every need of yours according to his riches in glory in Christ Jesus" (Phil 4:19)

If you come to Christ, you will never be insecure. You will have no reason to be anxious about the present or fearful about the future. You will not need to have a miserable, compulsive lifestyle. You won't need to be legalistic about rules and regulations. You won't need to amass wealth and possessions for protection.

This change will make you happier, and it will improve your relationship with others. A Christian conversion will make you a better mate, parent, friend, neighbor, and citizen because you won't be reacting in destructive ways to achieve security.

The salvation story is designed to turn insecurity into security. If you come to Christ, you are secure forever. That's the gospel, and that's why the salvation experience makes a difference in your life.

Forgiveness

A salvation experience makes a tangible difference in a person's life. The experience makes a difference because it fills basic human needs, and when these needs are filled, negative urges and reactions are abolished. For instance, when we are guilty, the resentment we feel causes us to react in destructive ways. But when we realize that God's forgiveness is absolute, these problems are eliminated. This change is called conversion.

God knows we yearn for forgiveness. Jesus said, "Your Father knows what you need before you ask him" (Matt 6:8). Jesus himself was accused of guilt. The scriptures say, "Then the high priest tore his clothes and said, 'He has blasphemed! Why do we still need witnesses? You have now heard his blasphemy. What is your verdict?' They answered, 'He deserves death'" (Matt 26:65–66).

He was also perceptive. Scripture says, "Jesus…needed no one to testify about anyone; for he himself knew what was in everyone" (John 2:24–25). This means he understood the deep psychological needs and problems of human beings.

The Need for Forgiveness

We are born with survival instincts that tend to make us egocentric and defensive. Furthermore, we all grow up in imperfect environments.

It's obvious that all of us have guilt. In fact, guilt can be helpful when it warns us about errors in judgment and encourages us to correct our problems. Guilt is to our emotional and spiritual selves what pain is to our physical selves. It tells us something is wrong and makes us willing to change our attitude and behavior. If you are touching a hot stove, pain makes you move away, but after it's done its job, then further pain is unnecessary and unproductive.

Likewise, guilt is harmful and debilitating when we allow it to ruin our lives and the lives of those around us. Everyone needs forgiveness because everyone makes mistakes. We are all frail and flawed human beings. All of us hurt our loved ones. All of us do dangerous and destructive things. We think bad thoughts. We say harmful words. We do cruel deeds. In these cases, guilt is legitimate. It motivates us to improve our behavior. But sometimes we are blamed for things that are not our fault. Other people who are trying to exonerate their own guilt and defend themselves may try to project their feelings onto us. The Pharisees did that to Jesus, but he refused to accept the accusation, saying, "Which of you convicts me of sin? If I tell the truth, why do you not believe me?" (John 8:46). In other words, he was saying, "You're not going to lay a guilt trip on me." We may listen and evaluate advice or criticism, but in the end each of us is only accountable to our own conscience.

Many of us take responsibility for things beyond our control. When it comes to our obligations to others, what do our duties to our fellow men include? It's hard to draw the line. But we are not accountable for "fixing" other people's personal lives. We are not accountable for feeding lazy idlers. We are not accountable for protecting reckless risk-takers. We must recognize and accept our limitations without feeling guilty about it. We are always our brother's brother, but we are not always our brother's keeper.

Children, especially, take on these burdens. One child who had just had a tantrum when an eclipse occurred cried, "Oh, Mommy, I've killed the sun!" Girls and boys often feel that they caused events like the divorce of their parents or the death of a sibling. Unfortunately, most of us become guilt-ridden quite early in life. We begin to believe that accidents and tragedies are punishments for our sins. Some people even think they deserve abuse and failure.

Effects of Guilt

Guilt hurts so much that most of us try desperately to obtain forgiveness. In order to do this, we may deny our culpability and make excuses. We may refuse to accept responsibility for our own choices and behavior. We may blame others. We may point out the problems in our associates' lives. As Jesus said, we criticize "the speck in [our] neighbor's eye" in order to ignore the beam in our own (see Matt 7:3). Living with guilt makes us feel so miserable that we become negative, critical, and bitter. We become judgmental. We hold on to grudges and seek revenge.

On the other hand, some people internalize the problem. They punish themselves with stress-related illnesses. They sabotage their projects because they don't believe they deserve success. All of these undesirable actions are vain attempts to escape guilt and gain the forgiveness we need.

How Does God Fill Our Need for Forgiveness?

In one Bible story Jesus gave a prostitute the gift of absolute forgiveness, and she is still being remembered and honored today. This illustrates how salvation can make a tangible difference in a life. Scripture says, "One of the

Pharisees asked Jesus to eat with him, and he went into the Pharisee's house and took his place at the table. And a woman in the city, who was a sinner, having learned that he was eating in the Pharisee's house, brought an alabaster jar of ointment. She stood behind him at his feet, weeping, and began to bathe his feet with her tears and to dry them with her hair. Then she continued kissing his feet and anointing them with the ointment" (Luke 7:36–38).

When the Pharisee was critical, Jesus corrected him.

This woman was considered and treated as subhuman. Respectable women avoided her. Men wouldn't touch her in public. She was beaten down and guilty, but she showed great courage by daring to enter a Pharisee's house and actually minister to Jesus. Her tears, her deep sorrow, and her acts of sincere devotion showed her desire to have a different lifestyle. Jesus gave her the gift of forgiveness and praised her devotion, and this changed her life.

Notice that all these years of being isolated and demeaned and wallowing in remorse and guilt had not helped her in any way. It had not changed her or given her relief. Rather, it had forced her into a most unproductive lifestyle.

Imposing guilt never accomplishes redemption. It never causes people to improve. It never corrects their faults. Instead, it causes problems as we try to defend ourselves to escape guilt and gain forgiveness.

Our false beliefs about ourselves and God cause feelings of guilt that lead to resentment. But there is a remedy. John said, "If we confess our sins, he who is faithful and just will forgive us our sins and cleanse us from all unrighteousness" (1 John 1:9).

Since God knows our human condition, he created a plan to rectify the situation. This prostitute is an example of this miracle.

In Jewish society she was considered the lowest of the low. As a woman, she was judged much more harshly than a promiscuous man. They called her a wicked sinner and accused Jesus of sin simply for allowing her to touch him. They gave her no credit for her repentance, grief, worship, and generosity. But Jesus not only forgave her sins; he commended her and rebuked her critics. And his forgiveness changed her life.

Has Jesus's forgiveness of your sins changed your life? If you really believe Jesus's wonderful promise about forgiveness, it will change your life. Over and over, when Jesus saw a person's faith, he would say, "Your sins are forgiven" (Matt 9:2). This promise includes sinners of every description. No one is too damaged or too wicked or too late.

Unfortunately, even though God has forgiven us, too often we refuse to forgive ourselves. I once heard a preacher tell the story of a calf named Little Red:

> I had raised him, but twice he got loose, broke down fences, and ruined our garden. My dad was determined to get rid of him.
>
> One day, Dad was sending animals to the slaughterhouse. I was desperate and begged to save my pet. Finally, Dad said, "Okay, get him out of the pen, and I'll set him free."
>
> That was easier said than done. Even though Little Red was forgiven and free, he didn't know it, and he had no desire to leave the herd and go out into the green pasture by himself. Instead, he hunkered down among the doomed cattle and refused his pardon.
>
> I was frantic to save him, but he didn't understand my explanations. Fortunately, just before the trucks left, I was able to persuade Little Red to accept the forgiveness that was his.

That's our story. All of us have troubled pasts. All of us have regrets and remorse. All of us have made mistakes. All of us have deep needs that must be filled. But there is an answer to our questions. There is a solution to our problems. Paul said, "My God will fully satisfy every need of yours" (Phil 4:19).

If you come to Christ, you will never be paralyzed by guilt. You will have no reason to judge others. You will not need to live in denial or hold grudges or seek revenge.

This change will make you happier, and it will improve your relationship with others. A Christian conversion will make you a better mate, parent, friend, neighbor, and citizen because you won't be reacting in destructive ways to obtain forgiveness.

The salvation story is designed to turn guilt into forgiveness. If you come to Christ, you are forgiven absolutely. That's the gospel, and that's why the salvation experience makes a real difference in your life.

Guidance

A salvation experience makes a tangible difference in a person's life. The experience makes a difference because it fills basic human needs, and when these needs are filled, negative urges and reactions are abolished. For instance, when we are confused, the uncertainty we feel causes us to react in destructive ways. But when we realize that God gives us guidance, these problems are eliminated. This change is called conversion.

God knows we yearn for guidance. Jesus said, "Your Father knows what you need before you ask him" (Matt 6:8). Jesus himself knew what it was like to be guided by God. He prayed, "My Father, if it is possible, let this cup pass from me; yet not what I want but what you want" (Matt 26:39).

He was also perceptive. Scripture says, "Jesus...needed no one to testify about anyone; for he himself knew what was in everyone" (John 2:24–25). This means he understood the deep psychological needs and problems of human beings.

The Need for Guidance

We are born with survival instincts that tend to make us impulsive and shortsighted. Furthermore, all of us grow up in imperfect environments. Therefore, it's hard to make good decisions that will be best for everyone over the long term. Modern-day life is complicated. It's difficult to distinguish between black and white because situations and motives must be considered. For instance, is it right or wrong to throw a baby out of a second-story window? You can't even answer such a simple question with an absolute "Yes!" or "No!" It's wrong if a drunk guy does it in anger, but it's right if a fireman does it from a burning building into a net below.

We face so many choices every day that it's impossible to make perfect decisions. Then, too, we are conditioned from birth to obey and do as we're told. Later, these commands from others may not always be in our best interest. As children we're compelled to please parents and teachers and other authority figures. This makes us question our own feelings and opinions and desires.

Also, there are so few good role models today. Even family members fail us. Immature parents with their own problems are not good examples for children. Divorce, spouse abuse, and absentee fathers are common.

Many relatives have alcohol and drug addictions. Community leaders fail. Our political leaders are flawed.

But perhaps most damaging of all are our spiritual and religious leaders who have very public "falls from grace."

With the prevalence of the internet, television, and smartphones, diverse opinions and ideas can be overwhelming. There don't seem to be any absolute ethical standards that will guarantee successful results. Life is changing so fast. Moral principles and rules of conduct aren't consistent. What seemed proper for our ancestors no longer has meaning today. Our youth are in desperate need of guidelines

Effects of a Lack of Guidance

Confusion hurts so much that most of us try desperately to achieve certainty and avoid mistakes. To do this we may be paralyzed with indecision. We may procrastinate about choices. We may waste time and energy on ineffective and unproductive activities. We may start many projects and complete none. We may make serious mistakes through trial and error. Nothing satisfies! All of us tend to be impulsive and shortsighted. All of us are egocentric, always wanting our own way. We don't consider the big picture and the overall consequences of our actions. We don't know the future. We don't even have all the facts about the present. So we need advice. Too often, we turn to the wrong people for that advice. Popular opinion is flawed, and manipulators have their own agendas. Few people have our best interest at heart. So we flounder.

All of these undesirable actions are vain attempts to gain the certainty and receive the guidance we need.

How Does God Fill Our Need for Guidance?

In one Bible story a spiritual confrontation and words of guidance to Saul of Tarsus caused him to become a man called Paul. Later, he wrote half of the New Testament and revolutionized the world. This illustrates how salvation can make a real, tangible difference in life. The scriptures say,

> Meanwhile Saul, still breathing threats and murder against the disciples of the Lord, went to the high priest and asked him for letters to the synagogues at Damascus, so that if he found any who belonged to the Way, men or women, he might bring them bound to Jerusalem. Now as he was going along and approaching Damascus, suddenly a light from

heaven flashed around him. He fell to the ground and heard a voice saying to him, "Saul, Saul, why do you persecute me?" He asked, "Who are you, Lord?" The reply came, "I am Jesus, whom you are persecuting. But get up and enter the city, and you will be told what you are to do." (Acts 9:1–6)

After he met Ananias and was baptized, this former enemy of the gospel witnessed and preached. Scripture says, "He began to proclaim Jesus in the synagogues, saying, 'He is the Son of God'" (Acts 9:20), and the rest is history.

Saul was well educated and extremely religious, but his goals were misplaced. He was keeping the laws and practicing the rituals of his faith, but they were totally destructive. Furthermore, he actually believed he was serving God when he persecuted and murdered Christians. However, when he met Jesus and asked what he should do, the Lord gave guidance. Paul gives his own testimony, saying,

I am grateful to Christ Jesus our Lord, who has strengthened me, because he judged me faithful and appointed me to his service, even though formerly I was a blasphemer, a persecutor, and a man of violence. But I received mercy because I acted ignorantly in unbelief, and the grace of our Lord overflowed for me with the faith and love that are in Christ Jesus. The saying is sure and worthy of full acceptance, that Christ Jesus came into the world to save sinners—of whom I am the foremost. But for that very reason I received mercy, so that in me, as the foremost, Jesus Christ might display the utmost patience, making me an example to those who would come to believe in him for eternal life. (1 Tim 1:12–16)

Paul followed that guidance, and it changed his life.

Notice that all these years of trying earnestly to do the right things and being industrious and devoutly religious had not helped Paul in any way. It had not changed him or caused him to make good decisions. He had not become more tolerant or compassionate. Rather, it had forced him into a most hostile and unproductive lifestyle.

Good intentions never accomplish redemption. They never cause people to improve. They never correct their faults. Instead, they cause problems as we try to operate and get the guidance we need.

Our false beliefs about ourselves and God create feelings of uncertainty that lead to lack of productivity and waste. Paul finally realized his folly, saying, "I am the least of the apostles, unfit to be called an apostle, because I persecuted the church of God" (1 Cor 15:9).

Since God knows our human condition, he created a plan to rectify the situation. Saul of Tarsus is an example of this miracle. He was a dangerous and antagonistic enemy of Jesus Christ. He was working night and day to undermine the early church and destroy every aspect of Christ's message and mission. He was cruel enough to participate in the stoning death of the good man named Stephen. He was on a destructive path. His choices were wrong. His religious dedication, his theological expertise, his legal training, his education, and his good intentions were useless until he met the living Lord, and that changed his life.

Has Jesus's guidance changed your life? If you really believe Jesus's wonderful promise about guidance, it will change your life. He said, "When the Spirit of truth comes, he will guide you into all the truth; for he will not speak on his own, but will speak whatever he hears, and he will declare to you the things that are to come" (John 16:13).

This promise includes sinners of every description. No one is too confused or too impulsive. Paul's conversion is evidence that it's never too late for anyone to change.

Once, a little boy was lost in the woods. As it got dark, he huddled on the ground, uncertain, discouraged, and afraid. Eventually, he trudged on, hoping he would find a trail. But he only got deeper and deeper into a thicket.

Finally, he realized that he was hopelessly lost. It was cold, and he was hungry. There might be wild animals. In desperation he cried, "Help me! I'm lost!" Then, all at once, he caught a glimpse of a light in the distance. As he stumbled toward it, he heard a man's voice saying, "Stay where you are, son. I will come and get you."

He did as he was told, and soon he saw the gleam of a flashlight through the trees. Then a voice said, "Follow me."

Now, there were fireflies in the darkness and sounds of animals and insects all around. But the boy didn't follow them. He only followed the man with the light. And the man with the light led him to safety. Jesus said, "I am the light of the world. Whoever follows me will never walk in darkness but will have the light of life" (John 8:12).

All of us have troubled pasts. All of us have regrets and remorse. All of us have made mistakes. All of us have deep needs that must be filled. But there is an answer to our questions. There is a solution to our problems. Paul said, "My God will fully satisfy every need of yours" (Phil 4:19).

If you follow Christ, you will never be bogged down in confusion. You will have no reason to hesitate and procrastinate. You will not need to waste time and energy going down blind alleys.

This change will make you happier, and it will improve your relationship with others. A Christian conversion will make you a better mate, parent, friend, neighbor, and citizen because you won't be reacting in destructive ways without proper guidance. The salvation story is designed to turn confusion into certainty. If you come to Christ, you will have access to God's guidance through the Holy Spirit. That's the gospel, and that's why the salvation experience makes a difference in your life.

Support

A salvation experience makes a tangible difference in a person's life. The experience makes a difference because it fills basic human needs, and when these needs are filled, negative urges and reactions are abolished. For instance, when we feel weak, the helplessness causes us to react in destructive ways. But when we realize that God supports us, these problems are eliminated. This change is called conversion.

God knows we yearn for support. Jesus said, "Your Father knows what you need before you ask him" (Matt 6:8). Jesus knew what it was like to need support. The scripture says, "Then he came to the disciples and found them sleeping; and he said to Peter, 'So, could you not stay awake with me one hour?'" (Matt 26:40).

He was also perceptive. Scripture says, "Jesus…needed no one to testify about anyone; for he himself knew what was in everyone" (John 2:24–25). This means he understood the deep psychological needs and problems of human beings.

The Need for Support

We are born totally dependent. We cannot survive on our own. This tends to make us vulnerable and weak. Furthermore, we all grow up in imperfect environments. All of us feel helpless at times. It begins when we are tiny babies. Without the strength or resources to fend for ourselves, we must rely on our parents and other caretakers for life itself.

Parents tell us over and over that we can't do this and we're not big enough to do that. One child was frustrated when she was told, "You're not old enough to go to school." A few minutes later she was told, "You're too old to suck your thumb." She said, "Mommy, I just wish you'd make up your mind!"

As teenagers and even as adults we are often at the mercy of teachers, employers, bankers, public officials, policemen, and other people who control our fate. Government regulations and business bureaucracies are so complex. We feel helpless when we're caught in endless red tape. Legal issues are often unfair and complicated. Mindless rules and restrictions frustrate us.

Sometimes we get into situations and relationships that actually encourage us to be helpless. Unfortunately, some people are such controllers that they enable our dependence because they want to manipulate us. Others with good intentions use unproductive methods in misguided attempts to "take care of us." The youngest child or baby of the family is especially vulnerable to this treatment. None of these things are psychologically healthy. We were meant to be mature and autonomous individuals.

Even some religious teachings tend to keep us subservient. Emphasis on God's wrath and sovereignty often leaves us with the impression that he's a great egotistical monarch who desires submissive slaves. But God did not create us to be puppets or mindless robots. Instead, he created us in his image. He expects us to take charge of things and be good stewards of his beautiful world. The psalmist said, "What are human beings that you are mindful of them, mortals that you care for them? Yet you have made them a little lower than God, and crowned them with glory and honor. You have given them dominion over the works of your hands; you have put all things under their feet" (Ps 8:4–6). Later, he continued, "[The God of Israel] gives power and strength to his people" (Ps 68:35).

A healthy Christian belief must be based on scriptures like Paul's wonderful statement: "I can do all things through him who strengthens me" (Phil 4:13).

Effects of a Lack of Support

Feeling weak and helpless hurts so much that most of us try desperately to gain strength and independence. In order to do this, we may take the easy way by avoiding situations that require strength. We may be apathetic, refusing to become involved. We may shirk responsibility. We may claim to have no talents or skills. When asked to minister, we say, "Let George do it."

But hiding our light under a bushel is wrong. God wants us to show courage and persistence. Isaiah said, "He gives power to the faint, and strengthens the powerless" (Isa 40:29).

Sometimes, however, instead of acting helpless, we go to the other extreme by pretending to have super-strength. We may become a bully. We may try to take command of every project. We may try to take control of every group activity. We may dominate members of our family and associates.

All of these undesirable actions are vain attempts to gain the strength we need.

How Does God Fill Our Need for Support?

In one Bible story Jesus promised his support to his faithless and cowardly followers, and they became a powerful force for good. This illustrates how salvation can make a real, tangible difference in lives. The scriptures say, "Now the eleven disciples went to Galilee, to the mountain to which Jesus had directed them. When they saw him, they worshiped him; but some doubted. And Jesus came and said to them, 'All authority in heaven and on earth has been given to me. Go therefore and make disciples of all nations, baptizing them in the name of the Father and of the Son and of the Holy Spirit, and teaching them to obey everything that I have commanded you. And remember, I am with you always, to the end of the age'" (Matt 28:16–20).

Later, Scripture reassures us, "You will receive power when the Holy Spirit has come upon you; and you will be my witnesses in Jerusalem, in all Judea and Samaria, and to the ends of the earth" (Acts 1:8). This wonderful promise that we can receive power from outside ourselves provides us with one of the strongest assurances of divine presence: "Those who wait for the LORD shall renew their strength, they shall mount up with wings like eagles, they shall run and not be weary, they shall walk and not faint" (Isa 40:31).

We no longer have to run from trying situations or avoid difficult tasks. God assures us that we are able to handle life's difficulties. Paul explained this, saying, "God is faithful, and he will not let you be tested beyond your strength, but with the testing he will also provide the way out so that you may be able to endure it" (1 Cor 10:13).

Now, this group of disciples had completely failed and deserted Jesus. Some slept while he prayed. Some ran away. Some denied that they knew him. They all felt hopeless, helpless, and weak. They were hesitant to act and avoided any involvement on Jesus's behalf.

However, when Jesus promised his support and assured them of his continued presence, this changed their lives. They became dedicated servants, enduring persecution and even sacrificing their lives for the cause of Christ. They were able to say with Paul, "If God is for us, who is against us?" (Rom 8:31).

Notice that all these years of being weak and dependent had not helped the disciples in any way. It had not changed them or caused them to respond maturely. Rather, it had left them with a most unproductive lifestyle.

Being dependent never accomplishes redemption. It never causes people to improve. It never corrects their faults. Instead, it causes problems as we try to defend ourselves and gain strength and autonomy. Paul criticized immaturity, saying, "And so, brothers and sisters, I could not speak to you as spiritual people, but rather as people of the flesh, as infants in Christ. I fed you with milk, not solid food, for you were not ready for solid food. Even now you are still not ready, for you are still of the flesh. For as long as there is jealousy and quarreling among you, are you not of the flesh, and behaving according to human inclinations? For when one says, 'I belong to Paul,' and another, 'I belong to Apollos,' are you not merely human?" (1 Cor 3:1–4).

God wants us to be mature and courageous. Paul said, "Keep alert, stand firm in your faith, be courageous, be strong" (1 Cor 16:13).

Our false beliefs about ourselves and God create feelings of weakness that lead to helplessness and apathy. Jesus knew what his disciples needed and said, "I am sending upon you what my Father promised; so stay here in the city until you have been clothed with power from on high" (Luke 24:49).

Since God knows our human condition, he created a plan to rectify the situation. The disciples are an example of this miracle. They had followed Jesus for three years. They had heard him speak. They had witnessed his good deeds. They had seen his wonderful works. He had promised them they would do even greater things (see John 14:12). But they still didn't understand. They slept while he prayed. They deserted him in his hour of trial. They ran away after his crucifixion.

Finally, when they understood his promise of personal support, it gave them strength and courage, and it changed their lives.

Has Jesus's support changed your life? If you really believe Jesus's wonderful promise about support, it will change your life. He said, "I am with you always, to the end of the age" (Matt 28:20).

The writer of Hebrews reminds us that God has said, "I will never leave you or forsake you" (Heb 13:5). This promise includes sinners of every description. No one is too damaged, too weak, or too late.

Years ago, a young man got a job in a city several miles from his home. He walked back and forth on weekends to help on the farm. Unfortunately, he had to cross a dangerous valley full of jagged rocks, thickets, howling wolves, and bandits' hideouts. The journey wasn't too bad in daylight, but once the youth was delayed at work, and he knew he would reach that valley after dark. Oh, how he dreaded the crossing. He was becoming more and more terrified as he approached the area. Then, out of the blackness he heard footsteps and a strange noise. He was panic-stricken until he suddenly heard his father's voice saying, "Son, I came to walk with you through the valley. You won't have to cross it alone."

What a tremendous difference that made. This story describes our situation.

All of us have troubled pasts. All of us have regrets and remorse. All of us have made mistakes. All of us have felt helpless. All of us have deep needs that must be filled. But there is an answer to our questions. There is a solution to our problems. Paul said, "My God will fully satisfy every need of yours" (Phil 4:19).

If you come to Christ, you will never be helpless. You will have no reason to fear weakness. You will not need to be apathetic.

This change will make you happier, and it will improve your relationship with others. A Christian conversion will make you a better mate, parent, friend, neighbor, and citizen because you won't be reacting in destructive ways to gain support.

The salvation story is designed to turn weakness into strength. If you come to Christ, you will have constant support. That's the gospel, and that's why the salvation experience makes a difference in your life.

Purpose

A salvation experience makes a tangible difference in a person's life. The experience makes a difference because it fills basic human needs, and when these needs are filled, negative urges and reactions are abolished. For instance, when we are aimless, we become unfocused, and this causes us to react in destructive ways. But when we realize that God has a specific purpose for us, these problems are eliminated. This change is called conversion.

God knows we yearn for purpose and meaning. Jesus said, "Your Father knows what you need before you ask him" (Matt 6:8). Jesus knew what it was like to be focused. He said, "I can do nothing on my own.... I seek to do not my own will but the will of him who sent me" (John 5:30).

He was also perceptive. Scripture says, "Jesus...needed no one to testify about anyone; for he himself knew what was in everyone" (John 2:24–25). This means he understood the deep psychological needs and problems of human beings.

The Need for a Sense of Purpose

We are born with survival instincts that tend toward self-preservation and short-term gratification. We want what we want right now! Our purpose in life is not stamped on us at birth, and we don't come into this world with a set of instructions. We aren't born with the discipline and vision necessary to reach long-term goals. Furthermore, we all grow up in imperfect environments. Much of our learning has to come from trial and error.

Also, when we are young, parents and teachers tell us what to do. Later, counselors, advisors, preachers, and advertisers tell us what we ought to do. As minors we have to follow the direction of others. Most of us, even as adults, still feel the need to fulfill the expectations of our elders. Everyone thinks they know what's best for us.

Others may mean well, and we can listen to their admonitions and suggestions, but ultimately each of us must discover God's purpose for ourselves. Then, when we feel called to a certain path, we must follow it.

Sometimes our strengths and gifts are hidden or neglected. We may even be criticized or ridiculed for our special traits and desires. Boys may be mocked for their love of music or art. Girls may be taunted for showing aptitudes in technology or science. Few people spend enough time and study and prayer trying to understand God's special plan for their life. Finding our niche can be difficult. Too many of us use the wrong criteria in choosing careers and professions. We may take the easiest path and do what our family does or what our neighbors do. We may only consider the income or salary instead of the good we can do and the satisfaction we can receive by using our gifts and abilities. No one purpose is right for everybody. Each of us is unique.

Dulcimers are musical instruments. Handmade wood and shape determine their tone. When a craftsman and musician was asked which one is best, he answered, "No one is best. They each have a different, unique sound." That's the way we are. No one occupation or profession is best. Each of us has specific abilities that make certain types of careers right for us. Nevertheless, following God's leading in a confusing world is difficult.

Effects of Aimlessness

Aimlessness hurts so much that most of us try desperately to be productive. To do this we may attempt to stay busy, jumping from one project to another. We may begin many things and finish none. Or we may try to follow someone else's advice and accept jobs we are not fit for. This makes us miserable and inevitably results in failure. If we aren't following God's pattern for our life, we will eventually lose interest and drop out. After years of this, the frustration and lack of success causes us to be apathetic and negligent. A few people become so cynical and dissatisfied that they get into immoral or illegal activities.

All of these undesirable actions are vain attempts to discover the purpose we need.

How Does God Fill Our Need for a Sense of Purpose?

In one Bible story Jesus gave Peter a specific purpose, and he became the leader of the early Christian church. The Scriptures say, "When they had finished breakfast, Jesus said to Simon Peter, 'Simon son of John, do you love me more than these?' He said to him, 'Yes, Lord; you know that I love you.' Jesus said to him, 'Feed my lambs.' A second time he said to him, 'Simon son of John, do you love me?' He said to him, 'Yes, Lord; you know that I love you.' Jesus said to him, 'Tend my sheep.' He said to him the third time, 'Simon son of John, do you love me?' Peter felt hurt because he said to him the third time, 'Do you love me?' And he said to him, 'Lord, you know everything; you know that I love you.' Jesus said to him, 'Feed my sheep'" (John 21:15–17).

Peter had an impulsive and rather reckless personality. He vacillated between extreme devotion and impetuous and thoughtless decisions. He's the one who stepped out in faith, but then when he saw the wind and waves, he faltered (see Matt 14:28–30).

He was also the disciple who first testified that "You are the Messiah" and Jesus called him "blessed" (see Matt 16:16–17). But in the same chapter, Matthew tells how Peter misunderstood and rebuked Jesus when he spoke of his crucifixion. At that time, the Lord had to say, "Get behind me, Satan" (see Matt 16:22–23).

These incidents show that Peter meant well, but he didn't always follow through. He had good intentions but not enough discipline and perseverance. Peter had also boasted that he would stand by Jesus when push came to shove, even if everyone else deserted him. But then he failed, not only by standing far off, but by actually denying his relationship to Jesus, then lying and cursing to make things worse. At this point he had no purpose, no goal, and no hope. In desperation he reverted to his old life, saying, "I am going fishing" (John 21:3).

Even that was a total failure. Peter's life personified aimlessness. He blew hot and cold. He had total dedication at one point and utter deception at another. However, when Jesus took time to meet with Peter "one on one," giving him an overriding purpose, it changed his life.

Notice that all these years of being aimless and unfocused had not helped in any way. It had not developed his character or caused him to become dedicated and successful. Rather, it had caused him to develop a most unproductive and unsatisfying lifestyle

Aimlessness never accomplishes redemption. It never causes people to improve. It never gives permanent satisfaction. It never corrects their faults. Instead, it causes problems as we try to find our niche, reach our goals, and discover our God-given purpose.

Our false beliefs about ourselves and God create feelings of aimlessness that lead to waste of our time, energy, and life. Indecision and vacillation are deadly. Elijah once said, "How long will you go limping with two different opinions? If the LORD is God, follow him; but if Baal, then follow him" (1 Kgs 18:21).

James said, "the one who doubts is like a wave of the sea, driven and tossed by the wind; for the doubter, being double-minded and unstable in every way, must not expect to receive anything from the Lord" (Jas 1:6–8).

Jesus said, "No one can serve two masters; for a slave will either hate the one and love the other, or be devoted to the one and despise the other. You cannot serve God and wealth" (Matt 6:24). We need a steadfast purpose in life.

Since God knows our human condition, he created a plan to rectify the situation. Peter is an example of this miracle.

Has discovering Jesus's purpose for you changed your life? If you really believe Jesus's wonderful promise about purpose, it will change your life. He gave Peter a life goal, saying, "Feed my sheep." This was Peter's purpose. But God gives each of us a purpose: "I know the plans I have for you, says the LORD, plans for your welfare and not for harm, to give you a future with hope" (see Jer 29:11). This includes sinners of every description. No one is too damaged or too aimless or too late.

Years ago, a lighthouse keeper was hired to do one job. It was his responsibility to make sure the lamp was burning to warn ships of the dangerous rocky shore. One month, he used up all his oil on other projects and then forgot to replenish his supply.

"Oh well," he thought. "It might not storm tonight. There may not even be a ship coming this way. Besides, someone else will probably see to the oil by next week."

But no one else did! That was his job. He had one responsibility, and he failed. Without a light, there was no warning. A ship broke up on the rocks, and lives were lost.

Each one of us has a purpose. No one else can be at the right place at the right time with the right skills to do what you are called to do. If you fail to respond, that need will remain unfulfilled and lives will be lost.

All of us have troubled pasts. All of us have regrets and remorse. All of us have made mistakes. All of us have deep needs that must be filled. But there is an answer to our questions. There is a solution to our problems. Paul said, "My God will fully satisfy every need of yours" (Phil 4:19).

If you come to Christ, you will never be aimless. You will have no reason to waste your life. You will not need to be unfocused and ineffective.

This change will make you happier, and it will improve your relationship with others. A Christian conversion will make you a better mate, parent, friend, neighbor, and citizen because you won't be reacting in destructive ways to discover a purpose.

The salvation story is designed to turn aimlessness into purpose. If you come to Christ, you are given a purpose in life; you'll have a mission to fulfill. That's the gospel, and that's why the salvation experience makes a difference in your life.

Hope

A salvation experience makes a tangible difference in a person's life. The experience makes a difference because it fills basic human needs, and when these needs are filled, negative urges and reactions are abolished. For instance, when we are in despair, the hopelessness we feel causes us to react in destructive ways. But when we realize that God gives hope, these problems are eliminated. This change is called conversion.

God knows we yearn for hope. Jesus said, "Your Father knows what you need before you ask him" (Matt 6:8). Even Jesus knew what it was like to feel despair. Isaiah said, "He was despised and rejected by others; a man of suffering and acquainted with infirmity" (Isa 53:3).

He was also perceptive. Scripture says, "Jesus…would not entrust himself to them, because he knew all people and needed no one to testify about anyone; for he himself knew what was in everyone" (John 2:24–25). This means he understood the deep psychological needs and problems of human beings.

The Need for Hope

We are born with survival instincts that tend to make us selfish and defensive. Disappointments occur, and we're helpless to control our future. Furthermore, we all grow up in imperfect environments. As children we have desires that are disregarded. We have yearnings that are ignored. We have needs that are unfulfilled. We have wishes that never come true.

Later, we see movies and soap operas and read romance novels. In this imaginary world everything is always rosy and perfect. When life isn't like that, we become disillusioned. Commercials show gadgets that work miracles in the kitchen, but when we order them, they don't live up to their claims.

Many factors add to our sense of hopelessness. The news is almost always bad. We only hear about violence and crime. Good deeds and pleasant occurrences are rarely noticed by the media.

Even religion can create disappointment. We may be led to believe that God is like a genie or Santa Claus. All we have to do is push a "prayer button" and everything will be miraculously fixed. Life will be wonderful. But Scripture never promised that. Jesus plainly stated, "In the world you face persecution" (John 16:33).

The gospel doesn't give us a fairy-tale existence. But it does give us hope. Paul said, "We do not want you to be uninformed, brothers and sisters, about those who have died, so that you may not grieve as others do who have no hope" (1 Thess 4:13).

If you lose hope, you stop caring and trying. As Christians we have an obligation to extend hope. Hope helps to dilute the misery in the world.

Effects of Hopelessness

Living in despair hurts so much that most of us try desperately to be optimistic and hopeful. But, realistically, life is hard. As we live and grow older, bad things happen. We suffer losses, we lose our health, and we age.

Lack of hope leads to depression. This has harmful effects on us physically, emotionally, and spiritually. Distress and sadness affect our brain chemicals and compromise our immune system.

In an effort to cope, we may clown and joke. We may pretend we're fine and cover up our feelings. We may put on a happy face. Such hypocrisy leads to stress and suffering.

Some people go to the other extreme, wallowing in self-pity or becoming severely despondent and giving up on life. Such despair is an unproductive and dangerous state of mind. It ruins relationships. It destroys families. It creates business failures. It can even result in suicide.

All of these undesirable actions are vain attempts to gain the hope we need.

How Does God Fill Our Need for Hope?

In one Bible story Jesus gives hope to a person who has run out of hope—the thief on the cross. The scriptures say, "Two others also, who were criminals, were led away to be put to death with him. When they came to the place that is called The Skull, they crucified Jesus there with the criminals, one on his right and one on his left" (Luke 23:32–33).

Both Jesus and the thieves are hours from death, but still there was hope. This illustrates how salvation can make a tangible difference in a person's life. The scriptures describe this tragic yet hopeful experience, showing how something very good can come out of something very bad:

> The soldiers also mocked him, coming up and offering him sour wine, and saying, "If you are the King of the Jews, save yourself!" There was also an inscription over him, "This is the King of the Jews." One of the criminals who were

hanged there kept deriding him and saying, "Are you not the Messiah? Save yourself and us!" But the other rebuked him, saying, "Do you not fear God, since you are under the same sentence of condemnation? And we indeed have been condemned justly, for we are getting what we deserve for our deeds, but this man has done nothing wrong." Then he said, "Jesus, remember me when you come into your kingdom." He replied, "Truly I tell you, today you will be with me in Paradise." (Luke 23:36–43)

This is perhaps the most dramatic biblical example of a conversion. Time had run out. This thief had been tried, convicted, and was already in the process of being executed. He had no time to go to church. He had no time to be baptized. He had no time to do good deeds. He seemed to be an absolutely hopeless case, but a tiny spark of hope remained. At the very last moment of his existence, this wretched man reached out with a faint expectation of response. Surprisingly, Jesus gave this seemingly worthless, wicked scrap of humanity the promise of paradise, and that changed his life and his future.

Notice that all those years of being miserable and hopeless had not helped him in any way. It had not changed him or caused him to repent. Rather, it had forced him into a most unproductive lifestyle

Despair never accomplishes redemption. It never causes people to improve. It never corrects their faults. Instead, it causes problems as we try to defend ourselves and reach out for hope.

Our false beliefs about ourselves and God create feelings of hopelessness that leads to despair. Job expresses this emotional state: "I loathe my life; I will give free utterance to my complaint; I will speak in the bitterness of my soul" (Job 10:1). Solomon said, "Hope deferred makes the heart sick" (Prov 13:12).

Since God knows our human condition, he created a plan to rectify the situation. The thief on the cross is a good example of this miracle. This man was a criminal. There's no question about it. Furthermore, only those who were considered the most dangerous and harmful criminals were crucified. People who want vicious robbers and murderers to be punished would have been totally correct in demanding the death penalty. If fairness was considered, he deserved his fate. Revenge seemed to be appropriate for the deeds he had done. He even admitted that his sentence was justified. But Jesus had a different attitude. He never hesitated or weighed his crimes. Instead, he simply extended mercy. He was putting the following scripture into practice: "God did not send the Son into the world to condemn the world, but in order that the world might be saved through him" (John 3:17).

This New Testament story was given to us to show that no one is too damaged, too wicked, or too late to benefit from God's promise of forgiveness and salvation.

Has Jesus's offer of hope changed your life? If you really believe Jesus's wonderful promise about hope, it will change your life. When the thief asked for help, the Lord made an immediate and unquestioned response. He was demonstrating the truth of his many earthly statements. Remember, Jesus had said, "Anyone who hears my word and believes him who sent me has eternal life, and does not come under judgment, but has passed from death to life" (John 5:24).

Here, at the eleventh hour, Jesus was still fulfilling his mission as he had described it when he said, "The Son of Man came to seek out and to save the lost" (Luke 19:10). This promise includes sinners of every description. It's the same with us. The thief on the cross had one possible opportunity, and he took it. Jesus said, "I am the way, and the truth, and the life. No one comes to the Father except through me" (John 14:6).

All of us have troubled pasts. All of us have regrets and remorse. All of us have made mistakes. All of us have deep needs that must be filled. But there is an answer to our questions. There is a solution to our problems. Paul said, "My God will fully satisfy every need of yours" (Phil 4:19). If you come to Christ, you will never be hopeless again. You will have no reason to despair.

This change will make you happier, and it will improve your relationship with others. A Christian conversion will make you a better mate, parent, friend, neighbor, and citizen because you won't be reacting in destructive ways to gain hope.

The salvation story is designed to turn despair into hope. If you come to Christ just as you are, you will be given hope. That's the gospel, and that's why the salvation experience makes a difference in your life.

Part 3:
The Church Must Promote
Abundant Life

A man recalled his 1951 Oldsmobile. It had been the latest thing in cars, but now it had no seatbelts, no airbags, no air conditioning, and no cruise control. What had been state-of-the-art in automotive technology then is now unacceptable.

It's the same with everything. Schools once had slates; now they have computers. People once had wood stoves; now they have microwaves. Groups sent smoke signals; now they have cellphones. Change is inevitable.

Jesus knew this. He constantly updated the rules and practices of the past, saying over and over again, "You have heard that it was said to those of ancient times.... But I say...'" (Matt 5:21–22, 27–28, 33–34).

Some of the laws he changed were actually Old Testament commandments supposedly given by God. Jesus realized that institutions must change as life changes. The church is no exception. It must relate to current situations. Tomorrow is never going to be like yesterday, and it shouldn't be. It's only the basic human needs that are constant. Jesus knew this, and he told us to fill those needs: "Go therefore and make disciples of all nations…teaching them to obey everything that I have commanded you" (Matt 28:19–20).

What are those universal needs that never change, and what did Jesus say about them?

Jesus accepted those who felt rejected.

In that culture, sinners, lepers, and foreigners were totally rejected, but Jesus said, "Everything that the Father gives me will come to me, and anyone who comes to me I will never drive away" (John 6:37b).

The church must do likewise!

A counselor said, "Every time I ask a successful person, 'When it's dark and you are alone, do you ever say to yourself, "What will I do when they find out who I really am?"' I've never failed to get a nod."

Why are we afraid others might think we're inferior and deserve to be rejected? Do you ever feel that you're not good enough? Do you ever feel that you don't belong? If so, your fears are shared by millions of people. The church of the twenty-first century must offer acceptance.

Jesus loved those who were different.

In that culture, Samaritans, Romans, heretics, and criminals were hated, but Jesus said, "Love your enemies, do good" (Luke 6:35).

The church must do likewise!

A man finally decided to ask his boss for a raise. He told his wife that morning what he was about to do. The man was nervous, but his boss agreed to a raise. The man came home to a beautiful table setting, complete with candles. His wife had prepared a celebration. Immediately, he figured someone from the office had called her about his good news.

When he told her, she handed him a card that read, "Congratulations, darling! I knew you'd get the raise! This dinner tells you how much I love you."

Later, when she went to the kitchen, he noticed that a second card had fallen from her pocket. Picking it up, he read, "Don't worry about not getting a raise! You deserve it anyway! This dinner tells you how much I love you."

You see, her love was absolute whether he experienced success or failure. That's the kind of love the church of the twenty-first century must give!

Jesus valued those who felt worthless.

In that culture, women, children, slaves, and handicapped people were despised and dishonored. But Jesus said, "You are of more value than many sparrows" (Matt 10:31). Jesus valued people.

The church must do likewise!

It's not your gender, or your race, or your occupation, or your wealth that determines your worth; it's what's inside of you. The church of the twenty-first century must value people because they are God's creation with immortal souls.

Jesus offered security to those who felt insecure.

Even religious men and women of the first century were constantly afraid of angering the deities. They feared the wrath of God. But Jesus said, "Not a hair of your head will perish" (Luke 21:18). He guaranteed protection.

The church must do likewise!

Some biologists in the Alps saw a rare plant down in a deep, rocky crevice. They offered a little shepherd boy money to go down to get it. They promised to tie a rope around him as a safety measure. He looked at the dangerous cliff and refused. Finally, when he saw his dad coming across the field, he made a decision. "Okay," he told the men, "I'll do it! But only if you'll let my father hold that rope."

The church of the twenty-first century must assure people that God can be trusted to hold the rope.

Jesus forgave those who felt guilty.

In those days, forgiveness was only offered after penance and retribution. But Jesus said, "Whenever you stand praying, forgive, if you have anything against anyone; so that your Father in heaven may also forgive you your trespasses" (Mark 11:25).

Jesus even forgave those who crucified him, saying, "Father, forgive them; for they do not know what they are doing" (Luke 23:34).

The church must do likewise!

Years ago, a child with learning disabilities was kept after school. He was told to write his spelling words and work his math problems on the chalkboard. He did his best, but every word was misspelled, and every addition column was incorrect. He dreaded morning when he knew the teacher would scold and the pupils would laugh. But when he arrived the next day, to his great joy he found that the cleaning crew had wiped the board clean. No mistakes remained.

The church of the twenty-first century must assure people that's what God does for us.

Jesus gave guidance to those who felt uncertain.

Uncertainty is paralyzing! In the first century, and even today, people waste time and energy making poor decisions, but Jesus said, "When the Spirit of truth comes, he will guide you into all the truth" (John 16:13). The Holy Spirit guides us.

The church must do likewise!

Whether you're lost in the jungle, on the streets of New York City, or on a raft in the middle of the Pacific Ocean, being lost is a terrible feeling. Being lost in life is also a terrible feeling. When we're unsure what decision to make or what road to take or which person to trust, we experience anxiety and depression. A map or an internal guidance system brings relief. That's what the scriptures and the Holy Spirit do.

The church of the twenty-first century must provide guidance.

Jesus gave support to those who were weak.

In Bible times, family members helped each other. However, help wasn't usually offered to strangers, as illustrated in the parable of the good Samaritan. But Jesus promised his presence at all times, saying, "I am with you always, to the end of the age" (Matt 20:28). Jesus supported his followers.

The church must do likewise!

A Jewish legend tells about a young leaf on a tree that wanted to be free. He was tired of being bound to the branch day after day. He wanted to fly on the wings of the wind and see the world. So he twisted and turned until he tore himself loose from the branch and soared off into space.

At first it was thrilling! He danced on the breeze and raced along the highways. He went everywhere a leaf wasn't supposed to go. But when night came, he lay alone among the garbage and shivered. Each day, he became weaker and weaker, until one day he curled up, turned brown, and died.

As Christians we must stay connected in order to help and encourage each other. The church of the twenty-first century must be a support group.

Jesus gave purpose to those who were aimless.

Being apathetic and unproductive is wrong. Jesus gave us a role to fill and a job to do. He said, "You will be my witnesses...to the ends of the earth" (Acts 1:8). He told his disciples it was their purpose to represent him and carry out his mission.

The church must do likewise!

Each of us has a niche to fill. Each of us has specific talents and abilities. But all of us are called to be witnesses. Edgar A. Guest said it this way in his poem, "Sermons We See":

> And the lecture you deliver may be very wise and true,
> But I'd rather get my lessons by observing what you do.
> For I might misunderstand you and the high advice you give,
> But there's no misunderstanding how you act and how
> you live.

The purpose of the church of the twenty-first century is to be a witness to the world.

Jesus gave hope to those who were hopeless.

People have always faced tragedies and disasters. Times have always been hard. Jesus said, "In the world you face persecution. But take courage; I have conquered the world!" (John 16:33). The gospel of Christ offers hope.

The church must do likewise!

Jesus said, "On this rock I will build my church, and the gates of Hades will not prevail against it" (Matt 16:18). Most of us think of this phrase in a defensive way, as if the church is so strong that Satan can't destroy it. That's true! But he also said we can be on the offensive. The church will be able to crash through the gates of Satan's strongholds. It may not happen in a day, but it will happen!

There is a legend about an old grandfather who, each day of his life, rose early and climbed to the top of a hill that blocked the morning sunlight. He would pick up a small stone, then walk back down the hill and drop the pebble on the other side of a stream near his home. Year after year, his sons and grandsons joined him in this task.

"Why do we do this?" one child finally asked.

The grandfather answered, "We're going to move this mountain!"

"But, Grandfather," the boy said, "you'll never live to see this hill moved."

The old man nodded, "Yes, I know that. But if you remain faithful, someday it will be moved!"

It's the same with Christian hope. The gospel promises victory! The twenty-first-century church will not fail! Evil will be defeated!

Acceptance

It's wonderful to feel safe and comfortable with a person—not having to pretend, not needing to weigh every word, and knowing that you are accepted just as you are.

People in our world today need acceptance.

Have you ever felt rejected? Maybe you were the last kid picked to be on a baseball team. Maybe you only got two valentines when all of your classmates got thirty. Maybe you were not given that scholarship you applied for. Maybe you didn't get the job after you sent in a résumé and interviewed. Maybe you couldn't get a date for the prom. Maybe your girlfriend refused your offer of marriage. From childhood and throughout our lives, countless incidents will make us feel unwanted and inferior. There are so many times and so many places when we just don't seem to fit in. Such things may seem insignificant, but rejection hurts.

Sometimes people who feel rejected become despondent or bitter. Many drop out of society. They may avoid the risk of applying for a job or entering into a relationship. This can lead to health issues, social problems, and even crimes. Jesus knew that acceptance is a deep universal need. That's why he said, "Anyone who comes to me I will never drive away" (John 6:37).

Jesus not only expressed acceptance in words; he demonstrated it. He touched lepers whom others shunned. He complimented Romans who were often despised. He praised Samaritans who were hated and ridiculed. He talked to women who were considered second-class citizens. He rebuked those who disregarded children (see Matt 19:13–14). He went home and ate with a well-known cheat and traitor named Zacchaeus.

Jesus also told a story about the importance of acceptance:

> Someone gave a great dinner and invited many. At the time for the dinner he sent his slave to say to those who had been invited, "Come; for everything is ready now." But they all alike began to make excuses. The first said to him, "I have bought a piece of land, and I must go out and see it; please accept my regrets." Another said, "I have bought five yoke of oxen, and I am going to try them out; please accept my regrets." Another said, "I have just been married, and therefore I cannot come."

So the slave returned and reported this to his master. Then the owner of the house became angry and said to his slave, "Go out at once into the streets and lanes of the town and bring in the poor, the crippled, the blind, and the lame." And the slave said, "Sir, what you ordered has been done, and there is still room." Then the master said to the slave, "Go out into the roads and lanes, and compel people to come in, so that my house may be filled." (Luke 14:16–23)

This story clearly shows that God's invitation excludes no one. The host sent his servant into the slums and red-light districts of the city. He didn't pick and choose the better neighborhoods. Alcoholics, beggars, and handicapped men and women were included. Then he went out into the rural areas and broadcast his offer. He didn't select his guests on the basis of prestige, popularity, or wealth. He didn't favor certain races or religions. The generous invitations of this man illustrate total acceptance.

The church of the twenty-first century must fill this need for acceptance.

Every organization, program, and service of the Lord's church must offer acceptance. Unfortunately, that hasn't always been the case. Too often, religions, denominations, and churches have been exclusive, giving the impression that only good people, proper people, pious people, or people like us are welcome. As a result, truly needy individuals have often avoided the church because they fear rejection and judgment.

Jesus had to remind people that this is wrong: "I have come to call not the righteous but sinners" (Mark 2:17).

An accepting church has a certain atmosphere. It's open and friendly. It emphasizes fellowship. It reaches out to the community. It involves many non-church children in Vacation Bible School. It encourages non-church families to attend social activities. It remembers shut-ins at Christmas with caroling visits and gifts. It provides funeral services and meals for relatives and friends during times of bereavement. This ministry is offered even to those who have not supported the church.

An accepting church performs weddings and baby dedications without demanding doctrinal conformity. It doesn't deny any individual the right to partake in Communion. An accepting church is tolerant because it realizes that rejection never accomplishes anything. Instead, those who feel hurt or ostracized become harder to reach. What's worse, one bad experience can create a negative attitude toward Christianity that is then passed on to future generations. Many people do not come to church because a grandfather or other ancestor was hurt by rejection.

In short, a church that is accepting has open doors to all mankind.

Zacchaeus was one of the most unpopular figures in his area. He was a Jew who had become a traitor to his neighbors and associates. He worked for the enemy and took unfair amounts of taxes from the poor. He cheated everyone for his own gain. He was truly a despicable character. Yet Jesus saw something else. He saw the person within. He saw the potential. So he stopped and called him by name. He went to eat with him, which in that culture indicated full equality and acceptance. As a result Zacchaeus totally changed. He repented and offered to make restitution: "Half of my possessions, Lord, I will give to the poor; and if I have defrauded anyone of anything, I will pay back four times as much" (Luke 19:8).

What do you think would have happened if, instead of calling him by name and treating him as an equal, Jesus had stopped and condemned Zacchaeus? He could have listed his many sins and lectured him on his deceit and greed. This would probably have pleased the bystanders, but Zacchaeus would have been embarrassed. He would have become defensive. He would have tried to justify his former behavior. Almost certainly, he would have continued his deceitful lifestyle. Jesus knew there were plenty of sins in his life to criticize and judge, but he didn't do that because he knew acceptance works; rejection does not (see Luke 19:2–9).

That's why the church of the twenty-first century must be accepting.

In the story Jesus told about the banquet, the host welcomed all sorts of people to his celebration. He ate with those who would ordinarily have been ostracized and excluded from polite society. That's what Jesus did with Zacchaeus. We must do likewise.

Now, Let's Get Personal.

As individual Christians, we are the church, so how can each one of us offer acceptance to those around us who feel rejected?

Remember, Jesus accepted us, so we must pass that blessing on to others. John said, "Whoever says, 'I abide in him,' ought to walk just as he walked" (1 John 2:6).

First, our attitude must be one of acceptance. A humble attitude doesn't mean we devalue ourselves. Instead, it means we do not degrade or dishonor others. We must not look upon anyone else as lower than we are. Disdain doesn't always involve actual words or deeds. It can be shown through facial expressions, body language, and actions. People can feel our subtle disdain. So we can pray for humility. We can study the scriptures admonishing us to be humble. The psalmist said, "For though the LORD is high, he regards the lowly" (Ps 138:6).

Jesus said, "Blessed are the poor in spirit, for theirs is the kingdom of heaven" (Matt 5:3).

Later, he said, "All who exalt themselves will be humbled, and all who humble themselves will be exalted" (Matt 23:12).

He used himself as an example, saying, "Take my yoke upon you, and learn from me; for I am gentle and humble in heart, and you will find rest for your souls" (Matt 11:29).

Paul said, "As God's chosen ones, holy and dearly loved, clothe yourselves with compassion, kindness, humility, meekness, and patience" (Col 3:12).

In order to have a true Christian spirit, we can watch our speech to avoid verbal put downs and prideful expressions. We can quit treating people differently, based on their looks or beliefs or achievements. We can encourage, help, and welcome all people to our services.

In the story about the banquet, the host accepted all of his guests with a gracious welcome. He treated all of them with equal respect. We must do likewise.

One morning, as a couple prepared their cereal, the man said, "Honey, we have two bananas. One is quite brown, and the other one looks perfect, nice and yellow."

"Okay," said his wife. "Throw the brown one away, and we'll share the other one."

"But the one that looks bad might be good inside," he replied.

When they peeled the bananas, they found that the brown one was perfect inside and the yellow one was rotten all the way through. That shows how easily you can be fooled by appearances!

Too often, we judge people as we do bananas—by the way they look. When we meet people, we don't know their troubles or their strengths and weaknesses. We may decide we like or dislike them based on our first impressions.

When we're tempted to judge people, let's remember the bananas and realize that none of us can know what is inside another person.

Once, a congregation was upset when they learned that some immigrants from the Middle East were going to attend their church. One little boy heard his parents' conversation and was curious. At the service he looked around eagerly and finally whispered out loud, "Mom, where are the immigrants? I don't see any immigrants. I just see people."

That's all God sees. He doesn't sort and label us. Peter learned this lesson, saying, "I truly understand that God shows no partiality, but in every nation anyone who fears him and does what is right is acceptable to him" (Acts 10:34–35).

We can take three lessons from this message: First, realize that feelings of rejection are destructive. Everybody needs to feel accepted. Next, understand that the Christian church is the chief organization here on this earth to fulfill that need. Therefore, let's try to make our church more accepting. Finally, believe that acceptance is a gift from God to you. When you incorporate that feeling of acceptance into your own life, then you will be able to extend it to others, and this will eventually change the world. And that's the purpose of the church of the twenty-first century.

Love

Hal David wrote, "What the world needs now is love ... Not just for some, but for everyone." Surprisingly, those people who seem to deserve love the least are actually the ones who need it the most.

People in the world today need love.

There are so many needs in our world today, and one of the greatest is the need for love. Have you ever felt unloved? Maybe your family neglected you. Maybe no one listened. Maybe your friends deserted you in a time of trouble. Maybe, when you were lonely, no one cared. Maybe others didn't understand your problems. Maybe associates had hostile attitudes and said hateful words.

Lack of love hurts. Babies who aren't touched and loved actually wither away. Adults with no love in their lives do desperate things to compensate.

Jesus knew that love is a deep, universal need. That's why he said, "I give you a new commandment, that you love one another. Just as I have loved you, you also should love one another" (John 13:34).

Jesus not only expressed love in words; he demonstrated it. Scripture says, "[Jesus] went about doing good" (Acts 10:38).

In fact, Jesus described the ultimate expression of love when he said, "No one has greater love than this, to lay down one's life for one's friends" (John 15:13)

He loved his friends. He loved his enemies. He loved the unknown masses of uncaring people. Paul said, "But God proves his love for us in that while we still were sinners Christ died for us" (Rom 5:8).

Jesus also told a story about the importance of love and gave us a different definition of love:

> A man was going down from Jerusalem to Jericho, and fell into the hands of robbers, who stripped him, beat him, and went away, leaving him half dead. Now by chance a priest was going down that road; and when he saw him, he passed by on the other side. So likewise a Levite, when he came to the place and saw him, passed by on the other side. But a Samaritan while traveling came near him; and when he saw him, he was moved with pity. He went to him and bandaged his wounds, having poured oil and wine on them. Then he

put him on his own animal, brought him to an inn, and took care of him. The next day he took out two denarii, gave them to the innkeeper, and said, "Take care of him; and when I come back, I will repay you whatever more you spend." (Luke 10:30–35)

This story teaches us that real love is not just an emotion; it's an act. The Samaritan had no personal relationship with this victim. He didn't know him. He may not have even liked him, but he had concern for him as a human being. He was willing to spend time, energy, and money to help him. That's the kind of love we are commanded to show. This is an illustration of Christian love.

The church of the twenty-first century must fill this need for love.

Every organization, program, and service of the Lord's church must emphasize love. Unfortunately, that hasn't always been the case. Too often, religions, denominations, and churches have emphasized God's wrath rather than his overwhelming love. Leaders have used threats and fears to intimidate instead of showing compassion and concern. As a result, truly needy individuals have often avoided the church because they believe it wants to condemn and punish them. Evangelists don't realize that love is the most powerful influence. Jeremiah expressed it well when he wrote, "I have loved you with an everlasting love; therefore I have continued my faithfulness to you" (Jer 31:3).

A loving church feels like a family. It truly cares more about individual men and women than it does about its own success and notoriety. It believes its main mission is to show its love through good deeds. Paul said, "Through love become slaves to one another" (Gal 5:13).

A loving church has benevolent projects that allow members of the congregation to share their resources. It gives people ways to channel donations of time, money, food, and clothing to those in need. A loving church plans worship services that emphasize the many things we have in common with other religious groups, rather than constantly pointing out our differences and criticizing those who disagree. A "holier-than-thou" attitude alienates visitors from other denominations.

In short, a loving church realizes that lack of love is the greatest evil. Hostility and negative attacks never influence anyone to become a Christian. Paul said, "The one who loves another has fulfilled the law" (Rom 13:8).

If we have to break a rule or change tradition in order to be loving, then we must do that. Paul continued, saying, "The commandments, 'You shall not commit adultery; You shall not murder; You shall not steal; You shall not covet'; and any other commandment, are summed up in this word, 'Love your neighbor as yourself.' Love does no wrong to a neighbor; therefore, love is the fulfilling of the law" (Rom 13:9–10).

Nicodemus was an upright, moral leader. He had respect and status in the community. In fact, he represented religion at its best. But something was lacking. Nicodemus came to Jesus privately, at night, to seek answers. Jesus often criticized Pharisees for their self-righteousness, and Pharisees often attacked Jesus for his unorthodox beliefs and behavior. But since Nicodemus was obviously sincere, Jesus spent time with him. He discussed his problems and answered his questions. He gave him the one secret ingredient that was missing in his theology.

It was to Nicodemus that Jesus shared the most famous verse in the Bible: "For God so loved the world that he gave his only Son, so that everyone who believes in him may not perish but may have eternal life" (John 3:16).

Later, we know that Nicodemus was truly changed, because he defended Jesus before the Sanhedrin when others wanted to kill him. This took great courage. Then Nicodemus helped in the burial of the Lord (see John 3:1–21; 7:50; 19:39).

What do you think would have happened if, instead of teaching Nicodemus and sharing the love of God, Jesus had shown hostility and treated him as an enemy? That would have been understandable since most Pharisees hated Jesus. But he didn't do that because he knew love works; hostility does not.

That's why the church of the twenty-first century must be loving.

In the story Jesus told about the good Samaritan, he described how he showed his love to a stranger even though it was an inconvenience and even though it required a lot of his time, energy, and money. Jesus treated Nicodemus with this kind of love. We must do likewise!

Now, Let's Get Personal.

As individual Christians, we are the church, so how can each one of us offer love to those around us who feel unloved?

Jesus loved us, so we must pass that blessing on to others. John said, "Whoever says, 'I abide in him,' ought to walk just as he walked" (1 John 2:6).

First, we must realize that love has hands and feet. John said, "How does God's love abide in anyone who has the world's goods and sees a brother or sister in need and yet refuses help?" (1 John 3:17).

The writer of Hebrews linked love to works: "Let us consider how to provoke one another to love and good deeds" (Heb 10:24).

Paul said it must be a growing love: "May the Lord make you increase and abound in love for one another and for all" (1 Thess 3:12).

Jesus commands us to love even our enemies: "Love your enemies, do good, and lend, expecting nothing in return. Your reward will be great, and you will be children of the Most High; for he is kind to the ungrateful and the wicked" (Luke 6:35).

This doesn't mean we must be affectionate with murderers and robbers, but it does mean we must have respect and concern for their welfare. We can have a caring outlook. We can be generous. We can be kind.

Love for others is our greatest witness and the greatest proof to the world that we are believers. Jesus didn't say people will know you're Christians if you have religious bumper stickers or say "Praise the Lord" a lot. Instead, he said, "By this everyone will know that you are my disciples, if you have love for one another" (John 13:35).

In the story about the good Samaritan, Jesus explained what Christian love is all about. The Samaritan showed concern and acted to aid the victim. We must do likewise.

The complete absence of love will destroy us emotionally, and in many cases physically. Once, families and close-knit communities provided this essential element of affection and compassion and concern. But today our impersonal world leaves little room for love.

The New Testament Christians emphasized fellowship and unity. In fact, love was the trademark of the early church. Unfortunately, in our churches today the primary focus is often on the weekly worship service and little else. Sometimes, especially in large congregations, the members do not even know each other. Worshipers desperate for real fellowship come and are given little or no opportunity to have interaction with others. The very structure of worship is performance, not community.

Our love for each other should be unconditional, as God's love is for us. He loves us in spite of our faults and failures. That's how we must love one another. True Christian love—God's kind of love—will ignore differences of color, race, denomination, and disposition. What a blessing our churches would be if all believers would learn to love one another as God has loved us.

We can take three lessons from this message: First, realize that lack of love is deadly. Everybody needs to feel loved. Next, understand that the Christian church is the chief organization here on this earth to fulfill that need. Therefore, let's try to make our church more loving. Finally, believe that unconditional love is a gift from God to you. When you incorporate that feeling of love into your own life, then you will find ways to extend it to others, and this will eventually change the world. And that's the purpose of the church of the twenty-first century.

Value

A famous poster of a little girl proclaims in big letters,
"God don't make no junk!"

People in the world today need value.

Have you ever felt absolutely worthless? Maybe you dropped out of school. Maybe you haven't achieved all you hoped to achieve. Maybe you realize you have a lot of flaws and weaknesses. Maybe you failed to complete an important project. Maybe you were fired from your job. Maybe you have suffered a divorce. Feeling worthless hurts.

Not being able to value yourself as a person is damaging and dangerous because you begin to live down to your evaluation. When you feel you don't merit respect and happiness in your life, then you will sabotage your endeavors. You will even stay in abusive situations because you think that's what you deserve. Since you no longer expect success or productivity, this sets up a cycle of defeat. Jesus knew that value is a deep, universal need. He said, "You are of more value than many sparrows" (Matt 10:31).

Jesus not only expressed value in words; he demonstrated his belief in others. He was the opposite of a prejudiced bigot. He touched lepers and outcasts. He talked to women. He held children. He spent time with tax collectors and Samaritans and Romans. All of these types of individuals were considered worthless in Jewish society.

The writer of Hebrews reminds us of everyone's inherent worth, reminding us not to judge from outward appearances: "Do not neglect to show hospitality to strangers, for by doing that some have entertained angels without knowing it" (Heb 13:2)

Jesus told a story about the importance of value: "Which one of you, having a hundred sheep and losing one of them, does not leave the ninety-nine in the wilderness and go after the one that is lost until he finds it? When he has found it, he lays it on his shoulders and rejoices. And when he comes home, he calls together his friends and neighbors, saying to them, 'Rejoice with me, for I have found my sheep that was lost.' Just so, I tell you, there will be more joy in heaven over one sinner who repents than over ninety-nine eous persons who need no repentance" (Luke 15:4–7).

This story is a dramatic analogy of the value of each individual. God doesn't see us as masses of humanity. He misses just one ordinary person. He grieves over the loss of even a single man, woman, or child. Furthermore, he never gives up. He searches until he finds the straying one. Then he celebrates when that lost soul is salvaged. This illustrates God's enormous concern for each one of us.

The church of the twenty-first century must fill the need for value.

Every organization, program, and service of the Lord's church must emphasize the value of individuals. Unfortunately, that hasn't always been the case. Too often, religions, denominations, and churches have elevated those with wealth and resources over those without such possessions. They have honored those in highly respected professions more than they have the unknown. They have catered to popular individuals rather than to the unpopular.

But Jesus actually did the exact opposite. He praised the poor rather than the rich. He praised the sinful publican rather than the self-righteous Pharisee. He praised the heretical Samaritan rather than the orthodox priests. He praised the servants rather than the masters. He summarized the infinite value of each soul by saying, "Some are last who will be first, and some are first who will be last" (Luke 13:30).

A church that values people is exemplifying the gospel. It has its priorities straight. It puts people over things. It helps each individual discover his or her own worth in God's eyes. It teaches principles that help people live moral lives. It offers excellent educational opportunities for those who desire learning and personal growth. It encourages leadership roles that make people feel productive.

A church that values people brings out the best in each member of the congregation. It honors those who have successes and those who receive awards. It especially gives approval and attention to young people who are good students and those who earn trophies or prizes. In short, the church that values people knows that appreciation for worth is extremely important because we live up or down according to our sense of worth.

Mary and her sister and brother were Jesus's intimate friends. Once, when he was visiting, Mary chose to sit and discuss theology with the Lord. Unfortunately, her sister, Martha, was displeased. She was cleaning and cooking and doing the regular chores expected of women. Seeing Mary sitting with Jesus made her angry. In the first place, this was unheard of in that day. Women were servants. Few were literate. Rabbis were forbidden to even teach them Scripture.

Additionally, Martha was probably resentful and jealous because she was having to do all the work. But when Martha challenged the Lord to make Mary fulfill her role and do her duty, surprisingly, he refused. Instead, he chided Martha, saying, "Martha, Martha, you are worried and distracted by many things; there is need of only one thing. Mary has chosen the better part, which will not be taken away from her" (Luke 10:41–42). Jesus knew that Mary's unique personality and intellect were just as worthwhile as Martha's.

What do you think would have happened if, instead of validating Mary's choice, Jesus had criticized her for not being feminine or not doing her duty? She would have been devastated, and today the women of the world would be poorer. He didn't do that because he knew giving each person a sense of value leads to success; devaluing them does not. That's why the twenty-first-century church must value every individual.

Remember, in the story Jesus told about lost sheep, the shepherd valued that one stray enough to leave the rest of the flock to seek it and save it. That's how the Lord valued Mary. And that's the way we must value each person in our church and in our community.

Now, Let's Get Personal.

As individual Christians, we are the church, so how can each one of us offer value to those around us who feel worthless?

Jesus values us, so we must pass that blessing on to others. John said, "Whoever says, 'I abide in him,' ought to walk just as he walked" (1 John 2:6).

First, we must look beneath the surface. We must not judge people by appearances, clothes, cars, houses, occupations, and possessions. We must avoid traditional prejudice and cultural discrimination. We must realize that Jesus died for all people. God loved the world, not just certain parts of it. Scripture doesn't say he values certain races or certain nationalities. Instead, it says, "For God so loved the world that he gave his only Son, so that everyone who believes in him may not perish but may have eternal life" (John 3:16).

Jesus said, "Do not judge by appearances, but judge with right judgment" (John 7:24).

Paul said, "Do not be haughty, but associate with the lowly; do not claim to be wiser than you are" (Rom 12:16).

He also said, "Love one another with mutual affection; outdo one another in showing honor" (Rom 12:10).

Later, he said, "For who sees anything different in you? What do you have that you did not receive? And if you received it, why do you boast as if it were not a gift?" (1 Cor 4:7).

Peter said, "Have unity of spirit, sympathy, love for one another, a tender heart, and a humble mind" (1 Peter 3:8).

We must find the hidden virtues in the immoral ones. We must uncover the latent talents in the nonproductive ones. We must encourage the use of the special abilities and skills in the neglected ones. Scripture says, "Exhort one another every day" (Heb 3:13).

In the story about the lost sheep, Jesus illustrated the inherent value of each individual. None were forgotten. We must do likewise.

Sometimes we don't stop to analyze how our speech affects other people. Once, a father and child were playing ball. The little boy said, "Look, Daddy! I catched it!"

His father said, "Yeah, but watch out. You missed that last one."

"Look, Daddy! I'm only eight, and I can throw faster than anyone!"

His father answered, "But your batting stinks, Tiger. You can't play in the big leagues if you can't hit."

"Look, Dad; I'm only sixteen and already made the varsity team."

His father responded, "You better do more practicing. Your defense still needs a lot of work."

"Look, Father; I'm thirty-five, and the company has made me vice president."

His father commented, "Well, maybe someday you'll start your own business like your old man; then you'll really feel a sense of accomplishment."

"Look at me, Dad. I'm forty, successful, well respected in the community. I have a wonderful wife and family. Aren't you proud of me now? All my life I've received everything but that one prize I wanted most—your approval. Just once I'd like to feel that I'm worth something. I'd like for you to put your arm around me instead of telling me I'm not good enough."

It's amazingly easy to destroy a person's self-concept, but exceedingly difficult to reconstruct it. Once we begin to think of ourselves as stupid, incapable, ignorant, and foolish, it's hard to change. Then, if we have problems in school, these feelings of worthlessness are increased. Failures build on failures. We all feel inadequate at times.

We can take three lessons from this message: First, realize that feelings of worthlessness are destructive. Everybody needs to feel worthwhile and significant. Next, understand that the Christian church is the chief organization here on this earth to fulfill that need. Therefore, let's try to make our church more positive and encouraging. Finally, believe that personal value is a gift from God to you. When you incorporate that feeling of value into your own life, then you will be able to extend it to others, and this will eventually change the world. And that's the purpose of the twenty-first-century church.

Security

People in our world today need security.

Have you ever felt insecure? Maybe your parents got divorced. Maybe you lost your job. Maybe your business went bankrupt. Maybe your home burned down. Maybe you were attacked or robbed. Maybe you have faced a serious health problem.

Insecurity hurts! Sometimes people who are insecure do desperate things in an attempt to seek protection. They may become victims of scam artists. They may join immoral groups or fanatic cults. Jesus knew that security is a deep, universal need. That's why he promised, "I am with you always, to the end of the age" (Matt 28:20)

Jesus not only expressed his promise of security in words; he demonstrated it. He was there for his disciples even after they deserted him. He was still there for Peter even after he denied him. He was there for Thomas even after he doubted him. He was there for the thief on the cross at the end of his life.

Jesus also told a story that proves his promise of eternal security:

> There was a man who had two sons. The younger of them said to his father, "Father, give me the share of the property that will belong to me." So he divided his property between them. A few days later the younger son gathered all he had and traveled to a distant country, and there he squandered his property in dissolute living. When he had spent everything, a severe famine took place throughout that country, and he began to be in need. So he went and hired himself out to one of the citizens of that country, who sent him to his fields to feed the pigs. He would gladly have filled himself with the pods that the pigs were eating; and no one gave him anything. But when he came to himself he said, "How many of my father's hired hands have bread enough and to spare, but here I am dying of hunger! I will get up and go to my father, and I will say to him, 'Father, I have sinned against heaven and before you; I am no longer worthy to be called your son; treat me like one of your hired hands.'" So he set off and went to his father. But while he was still far off, his father

saw him and was filled with compassion; he ran and put his arms around him and kissed him. Then the son said to him, "Father, I have sinned against heaven and before you; I am no longer worthy to be called your son." But the father said to his slaves, "Quickly, bring out a robe—the best one—and put it on him; put a ring on his finger and sandals on his feet. And get the fatted calf and kill it, and let us eat and celebrate; for this son of mine was dead and is alive again; he was lost and is found!" (Luke 15:11–24)

This classic parable leaves no doubt about the relationship between God and his children. That boy was his father's son before he demanded his inheritance and left. He was his father's son while he wasted his money. He was his father's son when he lived with the pigs. And he was his father's son after he repented and came home. His relationship with his father never changed. This is an illustration of the permanence of spiritual security.

The church of the twenty-first century must fill this need for security.

Every organization, program, and service of the Lord's church must promise security. Unfortunately, that hasn't always been the case. Too often, religions, denominations, and churches have left the impression that when a person falls or backslides or loses the joy of his salvation, he is to be condemned or shunned. As a result, many needy individuals have been turned away from the very source that should have helped them recover. This loss turns to resentment that goes down to future generations.

A church that provides security for its membership doesn't use fear tactics to ensure obedience and commitment. It trusts God and people enough to teach the biblical doctrine of assurance. It encourages morality, but it also stresses grace. We are not good, law-abiding, and dedicated to our church in order for God to save us and give us assurance. Instead, we are good, law-abiding, and dedicated to our church because God has saved us and given us assurance. Jude said, "To him who is able to keep you from falling, and to make you stand without blemish in the presence of his glory with rejoicing" (Jude 24).

People who are afraid of losing their relationship with the Lord are not free to serve. God doesn't want our obedience based on fear. He wants our obedience based on love. We increase our sense of security by developing self-confidence, by reading scriptures that promise the permanence of salvation, and by attending uplifting worship services. In short, a church that considers security as an essential element will find ways to reassure individuals through sermons, discussion groups, and individual counseling sessions.

The woman at the well was an insecure and confused soul. She had already married five husbands and was now living with a man who was not her husband. Because of this lifestyle, she would have been an object of ridicule. No proper women would have associated with her. Furthermore, she was a Samaritan. This hated group was avoided and detested by Jews.

She obviously had no consistency or stability or permanence to depend on. She was actually longing for something real and lasting. That's probably why she was so interested when Jesus said, "Everyone who drinks of this water will be thirsty again, but those who drink of the water that I will give them will never be thirsty" (John 4:13–14). She was so grateful for such a promise of security that she left her water pot and rushed away to tell others of this wonderful experience.

What do you think would have happened if, instead of interacting in a caring way with this woman, Jesus had lectured her on her immorality and shamed her for being a heretic? That would have increased her insecurity. Jesus knew assurance and security motivate people; fear and insecurity do not! That's why twenty-first-century churches must offer security for each individual.

Remember, in the story Jesus told about the prodigal, the father never gave up on his son. The moment the rebellious boy was willing, the father restored their fellowship. He put the ring on his finger as evidence that his status as a son and heir had not been nullified by his behavior.

In the meeting with the Samaritan woman, Jesus promised her this same sense of security. He told her she would never thirst again. We must give people that assurance and that sense of security.

Now, Let's Get Personal.

As individual Christians, we are the church, so how can each one of us offer security to those who feel insecure?

Jesus gave us the assurance of security. We must pass that blessing on to others. John said, "Whoever says, 'I abide in him,' ought to walk just as he walked" (1 John 2:6).

First, we must be secure in our own salvation. We must have assurance of God's presence in our lives. Then we must know what the scriptures say about a believer's security. Many scriptures tell of God's everlasting care. Solomon said, "One who trusts in the LORD is secure" (Prov 29:25).

Jesus said, "My sheep…follow me. I give them eternal life, and they will never perish. No one will snatch them out of my hand. What my Father has given me is greater than all else, and no one can snatch it out of the Father's hand" (see John 10:27–29).

In Hebrews, "[God] has said, 'I will never leave you or forsake you'" (Heb 13:5)

Paul describes the impossibility of God abandoning us. He says, "I am convinced that neither death, nor life, nor angels, nor rulers, nor things present, nor things to come, nor powers, nor height, nor depth, nor anything else in all creation, will be able to separate us from the love of God in Christ Jesus our Lord" (see Rom 8:38–39).

Later, he says, "By grace you have been saved through faith, and this is not your own doing; it is the gift of God" (Eph 2:8).

Our relationship with God is a gift, and God never takes back his gifts.

In the story of the prodigal son, we see that our behavior does not affect our relationship with God. It affects our fellowship. It affects our productivity. It affects our happiness! But nothing changes the fact that God is our father.

Birth is perhaps the most basic symbol of salvation. Jesus said, "No one can see the kingdom of God without being born from above" (John 3:3).

It's obvious that a child cannot be "unborn." It's also obvious that the parent and child relationship is an indissoluble bond. Furthermore, in this relationship, it's the parent who is responsible for the safety and well-being of the child. Some people say, "I'm afraid I can't hold out." Well, we aren't holding out. It is God who is holding on to us.

Rescuers pulling a baby out of a pit don't expect him to hold on to the rope. Instead, they go down and personally carry him out. Rescuers trying to save an injured victim floating in the ocean don't expect him to grab a lifeline. Instead, they fasten him so securely that the success of the operation depends upon the strength of the rescuer, not upon the strength of the victim.

In the matter of salvation, it's God that rescues and keeps us.

Once, a disturbed, insecure woman heard a preacher read this scripture: "The heavens will vanish like smoke, the earth will wear out like a garment, and those who live on it will die like gnats; but my salvation will be forever"

(Isa 51:6). She was greatly relieved. Unfortunately, when she awoke the next morning, the old insecure feelings began to return. Her little girl asked, "Mama, is that verse still there?" They got the Bible and looked it up.

There it was: "My salvation will be forever" (Isa 51:6).

"Then it's okay, Mama," the child assured her. "It's still true."

We can take three lessons from this message: First, realize that feelings of insecurity and doubt are destructive. Everybody needs to feel secure. Next, understand that the Christian church is the chief organization here on this earth to fulfill that need. Therefore, let's try to make our church more reassuring. Finally, believe that security is a gift from God to you. When you incorporate that feeling of security into your own life, then you will be able to extend it to others, and this will eventually change the world. And that's the purpose of the church of the twenty-first century.

Forgiveness

The most freeing thing a person can do is to just let go of his anger. Let the resentment fade. Let the bitterness ebb. Let the vindictiveness evaporate. Release the need for vengeance even when the scales don't balance, even when life is not fair.

People in our world today need forgiveness.

Have you ever felt guilty? Maybe you were disrespectful to your parents and now they are gone. Maybe you have lied to a friend. Maybe you did things as a teenager that you're ashamed of. Maybe you have addictive behaviors. Maybe you have been unfaithful to your mate. Maybe you have dishonored the Lord and damaged your witness. Everyone makes mistakes, but guilt hurts!

Many people feel so guilty that they punish themselves. They may feel they don't deserve happiness or appreciation. They may put themselves down and refuse to accept compliments. They may deny their accomplishments and sabotage their successes. They may become their own worst enemy.

Jesus knew that forgiveness is a deep, universal need. He said to the paralyzed man, "Take heart, son; your sins are forgiven" (Matt 9:2).

Jesus not only expressed the words of forgiveness; he demonstrated forgiveness. He forgave the woman caught in adultery and allowed her to go free. He forgave his disciples who slept while he prayed. He forgave Peter for cursing and denying him. He even forgave those who crucified him, saying, "Father, forgive them; for they do not know what they are doing" (Luke 23:34).

Jesus also told a story about forgiveness that may surprise legalists: "Two men went up to the temple to pray, one a Pharisee and the other a tax collector. The Pharisee, standing by himself, was praying thus, 'God, I thank you that I am not like other people: thieves, rogues, adulterers, or even like this tax collector. I fast twice a week; I give a tenth of all my income.' But the tax collector, standing far off, would not even look up to heaven, but was beating his breast and saying, 'God, be merciful to me, a sinner!' I tell you, this man went down to his home justified rather than the other; for all who exalt themselves will be humbled, but all who humble themselves will be exalted" (Luke 18:10–14).

This story epitomizes the doctrine of grace. It may be unnatural to let go of anger and bitterness. It may be hard to forgo revenge and retaliation. It may seem unfair for a faithful, law-abiding citizen, like the Pharisee, to leave the temple with his guilt unrelieved, while an obvious sinner, like the publican, is pardoned without punishment. But that's what happened. This parable is an illustration of absolute, undeserved forgiveness.

The church of the twenty-first century must fill this need for forgiveness.

Every organization, program, and service of the Lord's church must extend forgiveness. Unfortunately, that hasn't always been the case. Too often, religions, denominations, and churches have held people's pasts against them. Many congregations will not allow a person who's been divorced to serve as a deacon or minister. Also, some groups don't accept ex-cons or former alcoholics as Christian brothers and sisters. As a result, many needy individuals are excluded from the fellowship of the church.

A forgiving church does not categorize people into saints and sinners. It does not label people as good or bad. It truly sees others as God does. It sees them through the grace of Jesus Christ. It sees what they can be rather than what they have been.

Members of a forgiving church remember their own weaknesses and failures. They understand that all of us are under construction. All of us are being transformed. No one is perfect.

The forgiving church sees its role as a hospital for sinners. Congregations are here to offer healing and hope.

Sermons in a forgiving church deal more with compassion and pardon than with threats and blame. Most people already know they are sinners. They need someone to encourage their possibilities. In the Gospels we never see Jesus criticizing a sinner or kicking someone when they were down. His attitude and actions are to be our model.

In short, a forgiving church truly forgives. It doesn't keep digging up dirt and old sins. Instead, it sees converts as new people! Paul said, "If anyone is in Christ, there is a new creation: everything old has passed away; see, everything has become new!" (2 Cor 5:17).

Saul was a powerful enemy of the early church. He harassed, persecuted, and killed Christians. He participated in the stoning death of the devout believer named Stephen. Scripture says, "They dragged [Stephen] out of the city and began to stone him; and the witnesses laid their coats at the feet of a young man named Saul" (Acts 7:58).

Saul was an angry, vindictive individual. The scriptures say, "Saul, still breathing threats and murder against the disciples of the Lord, went to the high priest and asked him for letters to the synagogues at Damascus, so that if he found any who belonged to the Way, men or women, he might bring them bound to Jerusalem" (Acts 9:1–2).

If this man could be forgiven and changed, anybody can be forgiven and changed. Saul is now known as Paul, and he used his testimony for the rest of his life. He didn't deny it, cover it up, or excuse it. Instead, he plainly said, "I am the least of the apostles, unfit to be called an apostle, because I persecuted the church of God. But by the grace of God I am what I am" (1 Cor 15:9–10)

What if, instead of forgiving Paul, his murderous past had been held against him? We wouldn't have the blessings of Paul's great gifts. Paul is a dramatic example of grace and forgiveness. It's astonishing that God would forgive such a man and inspire him to write Scripture. That's why the church of the twenty-first century must forgive sinners.

Remember, in the story Jesus told, the publican was exonerated and justified without having to atone for his sins. That's what happened to Paul. That's the way we must forgive.

Now, Let's Get Personal.

As individual Christians, we are the church, so how can each one of us extend forgiveness to those individuals who feel guilty about their past? Jesus forgives us, so we must pass that blessing on to others. The scripture says, "Whoever says, 'I abide in him,' ought to walk just as he walked" (1 John 2:6).

First, we need to understand that our well-being rests upon our forgiveness of others. Jesus said, "If you forgive others their trespasses, your heavenly Father will also forgive you; but if you do not forgive others, neither will your Father forgive your trespasses" (Matt 6:14–15). This doesn't mean God withholds his forgiveness. It simply means that as long as we hold anger and bitterness in our hearts, we cannot receive and benefit from the Lord's forgiveness.

Jesus told Peter to forgive as many times as necessary: "Peter came and said to him, 'Lord, if another member of the church sins against me, how often should I forgive? As many as seven times?' Jesus said to him, 'Not seven times, but, I tell you, seventy-seven times'" (Matt 18:21–22).

He also emphasized that it's the role of the church to offer forgiveness. He told Peter he would build his church upon this principle, saying, "I will give you the keys of the kingdom of heaven, and whatever you bind on earth will be bound in heaven, and whatever you loose on earth will be loosed in heaven" (Matt 16:19).

Paul says, "Be kind to one another, tenderhearted, forgiving one another, as God in Christ has forgiven you" (Eph 4:32).

We must avoid gossip. We must change our judgmental attitudes. We must believe others have a right to leave their sins behind. We must give people a chance to start over and be free of their past. We must not label and stereotype individuals. We must realize that even criminals and thieves are more than that one act.

In the story about the publican and the Pharisee, Jesus explained that God forgives us before we make recompense or atonement. We must do likewise.

The ancient Romans had a gruesome way of punishing lawbreakers. The dead body of a victim was often tied to the body of the criminal. As the hot sun burned down, the body would begin to decay. Carrying such a burden totally incapacitated an individual. This is a perfect analogy of people who carry around loads of guilt. Paul must have had this in mind when he said of his own miseries and burdens, "Wretched man that I am! Who will rescue me from this body of death?" (Rom 7:24). Paul found the victory over his sin when he found Christ (see Rom 7:25).

Holding on to guilt is harmful and useless. Once, a minister visited two different families. Both had lost an elderly woman. At the first home the bereaved son said, "If only I had sent my mother to Florida and gotten her out of this cold and snow, she might be alive today. It's my fault that she died."

At the second house the bereaved son said, "If only I hadn't insisted that my mother go to Florida, she might be alive today. The abrupt change of climate was more than she could take. It's my fault that she's dead."

We mustn't blame ourselves or others for things beyond our control. That's assuming too much responsibility.

We can take three lessons from this message: First, realize that feelings of guilt are destructive. Everybody needs to feel forgiven. Next, understand that the Christian church is the chief organization here on this earth to fulfill that need. Therefore, let's work to make our church more forgiving. Finally, believe that forgiveness is a gift from God to you. When you incorporate that feeling of forgiveness into your own life, then you will be able to extend it to others, and this will eventually change the world. And that's the purpose of the church of the twenty-first century.

Guidance

William Cullen Bryant watched the geese fly south with no maps or compasses and marveled at the innate wisdom and guidance given by their creator. He closes his poem "To a Waterfowl" with these words:

He who, from zone to zone,
Guides through the boundless sky thy certain flight,
In the long way that I must tread alone,
Will lead my steps aright.[1]

People in our world today need guidance.

Have you ever felt confused? Maybe you couldn't decide about college. Maybe choosing an occupation or profession was hard. Maybe you didn't know whether to get married or join the military. Maybe finances are a problem and you don't know whether to rent or buy a house. Maybe you're facing moral or religious decisions.

Confusion hurts! Questions abound, and choices multiply. Life doesn't come with a manual or a guidebook. Most people muddle through year after year without focus or goals. They remain indecisive and uncertain. Such individuals are vulnerable to those waiting to exploit them and lead them astray.

Jesus knew that guidance is a deep, universal need. That's why he said, "When the Spirit of truth comes, he will guide you into all the truth" (John 16:13).

Jesus not only promised guidance with words; he demonstrated it. He taught, discussed, answered questions, gave advice. He used parables to clarify his teachings. He provided an example and a model, saying over and over, "Follow me." He encouraged his disciples to develop wisdom and autonomy. He tried in many ways to help people get their priorities straight.

Jesus also told a story about the importance of guidance: "Anyone who does not enter the sheepfold by the gate but climbs in by another way is a thief and a bandit. The one who enters by the gate is the shepherd of the sheep. The gatekeeper opens the gate for him, and the sheep hear his voice. He calls his own sheep by name and leads them out. When he has brought out all his own, he goes ahead of them, and the sheep follow him because they know his voice. They will not follow a stranger, but they will run from him because they do not know the voice of strangers" (John 10:1–5).

If we are able to really know the mind of Christ and tune in to the Holy Spirit's voice, we can learn to distinguish the true from the false. We will be able to tell right from wrong.

There are still "thieves and robbers" who try to lure unsuspecting people into destructive paths. Never before in the history of the world have we had so many conflicting messages coming at us. Radio, television, and internet offer varying interpretations. Temptations are rampant. Advertisers and propaganda can be convincing.

This story clearly shows that we can only be guided to make good decisions if we listen to the Holy Spirit within. It promises us that if we follow the example of the Lord and our own inner wisdom and good conscience, we can know what to say and what to do about important matters.

The church of the twenty-first century must fill this need for guidance.

Every organization, program, and service of the Lord's church must provide guidance. Unfortunately, that hasn't always been the case. Too often, religions, denominations, and churches have been dogmatic and close-minded. They've merely repeated creeds and listed doctrines instead of teaching people how to learn, how to think, and how to live. As a result, many Christians are brainwashed and conditioned to obey their leaders instead of becoming autonomous.

God gives us minds to think, and he expects us to use them. He gives us the Holy Spirit within. He gives us a conscience and common sense. He gave us the model of Jesus himself.

God's guidance does not consist of specific advice on every choice in life. He doesn't ordinarily tell us whether to eat blueberry pie or chocolate cake. Furthermore, God doesn't play games with us by hiding clues in strange places. God hasn't created us to be robots or game players or puppets. Instead, he has given us the right to act and make responsible decisions. In the scriptures "God said, 'Let us make humankind in our image, according to our likeness; and let them have dominion over the fish of the sea, and over the birds of the air, and over the cattle, and over all the wild animals of the earth, and over every creeping thing that creeps upon the earth" (Gen 1:26).

This shows that he has transferred much of his authority to us. We don't have to be afraid we're "playing God" when we make new scientific discoveries or create new inventions. That's our purpose.

For a church to provide guidance, it must be well organized. It must plan ahead. It must teach moral precepts. It must apply psychological principles. It must give practical help with self-discipline. It must counsel young people, married couples, and those with special needs. It must offer therapy to those with addictions. A church that guides will hold workshops on occupational choices and financial problems. Its educational programs will include classes and seminars on personal growth, social relations, and cultural issues. In short, a church that emphasizes reason and guidance doesn't just teach us what to think; it teaches us how to think. That's what makes the Lord's church different from cults.

Peter was at a crossroads in his life. He was confused and uncertain. Everything on which he had relied had collapsed. He had left his business to follow Jesus. He had truly believed the Lord would set up a kingdom and be victorious over the Romans. But then the worst happened when Jesus was arrested. Peter's faith disintegrated, and he began lying and cursing. After the crucifixion, when all seemed lost, Peter resorted to his past lifestyle as a fisherman, but that too was unsuccessful. Peter had hit rock bottom. He epitomized an uncertain, floundering individual with no idea of what to do next.

Eventually, Jesus talked to Peter personally and allowed him to express his devotion. Then he gave him a specific answer to his dilemma. He provided guidance for the future, saying, "I have a special job for you: Feed my sheep." If Jesus had condemned and shamed him for his unfaithfulness, Peter probably would have given up. Instead, he was able to preach a sermon a few weeks later at Pentecost that reached 3,000 souls.

The church of the twenty-first century must give guidance to each individual.

Remember, in the story Jesus told, he assures us that we can distinguish our shepherd's voice even when many other voices are clamoring for our attention. He says, "He knows us by name," and we can follow him if we listen and obey. Jesus gave Peter guidance, and it changed his life. The church must give guidance to its members.

Now, Let's Get Personal.

As individual Christians, we are the church, so how can each one of us provide guidance to those who are confused?

Jesus guides us, so we must pass it on to others. John said, "Whoever says, 'I abide in him,' ought to walk just as he walked" (1 John 2:6).

First, we must be mature enough to get our own priorities straight. We must be good decision-makers. We must model our life after Jesus. We must also know the scriptures well enough to use them in giving advice to others. David said, "I treasure your word in my heart, so that I may not sin against you" (Ps 119:11).

Solomon said, "Where there is no guidance, a nation falls" (Prov 11:14).

He also said, "Without counsel, plans go wrong, but with many advisers they succeed" (Prov 15:22).

Jesus emphasized the fact that one of our major responsibilities as Christians is to "feed the sheep"—to teach and share knowledge and information. Paul said we must "teach" and "urge" (see 1 Tim 6:2)—to give advice and counsel.

He also said we're to admonish one another: "I myself feel confident about you, my brothers and sisters, that you yourselves are full of goodness, filled with all knowledge, and able to instruct one another" (Rom 15:14).

We are God's messengers.

In the story of the sheep who hear the shepherd's voice, Jesus illustrates the importance of guidance. He helps us distinguish between the false and the true.

Once, a bridge was out on a major highway. The officials frantically broadcast warnings on the radio. A certain man heard and heeded the message and survived. Unfortunately, many other lives were lost. Most of those travelers either didn't tune in or else had heard the alert but didn't believe it. Why was one man saved when so many others died? Did God love him more than he did the victims? Not at all. A loving God plays no favorites. A loving God is no respecter of persons.

Just like the highway officials, God tries to reach us, but we may not be tuned in. Guidance may come to us in many ways, but we must be careful. In our complicated world we're open to many influences that are not from the Holy Spirit. These other sources can't be trusted.

Everyone has experienced thoughts and impulses that are selfish rationalizations or else are so wrongly motivated as to be evil. To be sure the voices we are following are of God, we must test them. John said, "Do not believe every spirit, but test the spirits to see whether they are from God; for many false prophets have gone out into the world" (1 John 4:1).

First, through prayer we can listen to inner urges. This is called intuition. Next, through Scripture reading we can discern understanding and reason. This is called insight. Finally, we can consider circumstances, possibilities, and good advice. This is called common sense.

It's especially important to realize that God's voice will never contradict itself. That is, he will not give us a direction through the inner voice that contradicts his voice in the scriptures. One lady stole some money because she had opened her Bible at random and put her finger on the words, "All things are yours," in 1 Corinthians 3:21. Obviously this woman should have considered the consistent voice of Scripture concerning honesty, for example, the commandment about stealing. The point is that the Bible deals in general moral principles, not disjointed sayings or superficial rules of conduct.

We can take three lessons from this message: First, realize that feelings of uncertainty are destructive. Everybody needs guidance. Next, understand that the Christian church is the chief organization here on this earth to fulfill that need. Therefore, let's work to help our church provide guidance.

Finally, seek God's guidance in your own life. Then you can provide guidance to others, and this will eventually change the world. And that's the purpose of the church of the twenty-first century.

[1]Published in *The North American Review*, March 1818.

Support

He gives more grace when the burdens grow greater.
He sends more strength when the labors increase.[1]

It's encouraging to know that even great souls reach places when they can neither go over, under, around, nor through. But by trusting God and then holding on, the difficulty can be overcome.

People in our world today need support.

Have you ever felt helpless? Maybe you need good advice. Maybe you are overwhelmed by a business problem. Maybe you encounter situations you can't handle. Maybe your friends and associates abandon you. Maybe you are facing several obstacles at once. Maybe you can't handle a frustrating relationship.

Feeling helpless hurts. No one is invincible. No one is all-powerful. No one is totally self-sufficient. All of us need assistance and backup. Life is hard. That's why Scripture says, "Two are better than one.... If they fall, one will lift up the other; but woe to one who is alone and falls and does not have another to help" (Eccl 4:9–10).

Sometimes when people feel inadequate and weak, they give up. Sometimes they allow controlling mates or associates to take over their lives. Jesus knew that support is a deep, universal need. He said, "The one who believes in me will also do the works that I do and, in fact, will do greater works than these.... I will not leave you orphaned" (John 14:12, 18).

Jesus not only expressed support in words; he demonstrated it. He helped his disciples in the storm. He fed the hungry. He answered prayers. He comforted Mary and Martha. He was always there for hurting people because he drew his strength from God. He said, "The Son can do nothing on his own, but only what he sees the Father doing" (John 5:19).

Jesus also told a story about the importance of support: "Abide in me as I abide in you. Just as the branch cannot bear fruit by itself unless it abides in the vine, neither can you unless you abide in me. I am the vine, you are the branches. Those who abide in me and I in them bear much fruit, because apart from me you can do nothing" (John 15:4–5).

Jesus knows we can't do everything alone. He knows that, as human beings, we need help. In order to withstand temptation, overcome obstacles, and be productive, we must stay connected to our spiritual support system. We can stay connected to God through prayer and reading Scripture, and we can stay connected to our Christian brothers and sisters through our church worship services and fellowship.

This story clearly shows where our strength comes from. It urges us to stay connected to God and other Christians.

The church of the twenty-first century must fill this need for support.

Every organization, program, and service of the Lord's church must give support. Unfortunately, that hasn't always been the case. Too often, religions, denominations, and churches have been self-satisfied. They have been content to simply enjoy worship and fellowship among themselves without reaching out to those who need help. As a result, the wider community, and especially the undesirable elements of society, do not get the aid they need to overcome negative factors.

Jesus reminds us that "just as you did it to one of the least of these who are members of my family, you did it to me" (Matt 25:40).

A supportive church builds up its members, and this in turn lifts the entire community and region. We're the "light and salt and yeast" in this fallen world. The church is there meeting needs during emergencies. It is there giving comfort during adversities. It holds people together through tragedies and misfortunes. It gives moral, emotional, and physical support. The church becomes a vital source of strength to help individuals and families through times of grief and crises. It may offer counseling sessions. Ministers, deacons, and members may visit and listen to people's problems. They try to follow Paul's advice: "Rejoice with those who rejoice, weep with those who weep" (Rom 12:15).

The church must view deaths and bankruptcies, divorces and illnesses as ministry opportunities. The church must have projects that channel donations to those in need. Ceremonial observances such as memorials and funerals provide important closure for grieving people. The sermons of a supportive church emphasize unity and optimism and faith. In short, a supportive church is a tower of strength to a hurting world. It draws its strength from God and passes it on to others. Jesus said, "On this rock I will build my church, and the gates of Hades will not prevail against it" (Matt 16:18).

Jesus exemplified a helping role and promised support. He reassured the group when they were afraid of the storm. He cared for the sick. He provided comfort to children. He wept with grieving people at Lazarus's grave. He sympathized with the grieving widow at Nain. Luke says, Jesus "came near the town gate, he saw a funeral. (She was) A mother, who . . . had lost her only son." When the Lord saw her, he felt sorry for her (see Luke 7:12–15).

Jesus encouraged the disciples when they returned from their first experience of preaching. Scripture says, "Jesus rejoiced in the Holy Spirit and said, 'I thank you, Father, Lord of heaven and earth, because you have hidden these things from the wise and the intelligent and have revealed them to infants; yes, Father, for such was your gracious will'" (Luke 10:21). Then he promised his continual presence when he gave the disciples the "great commission," saying, "I am with you always, to the end of the age" (Matt 28:20).

That's why the church of the twenty-first century must provide support.

Remember, in the story Jesus told, he explained how the vine is the source of power and wisdom. Each of us, as a branch, must stay connected in order to draw strength from the living vine. Without that connection we wither, lose our strength, and become useless. But if we stay connected, we will be able to give support to others.

Now, Let's Get Personal.

As individual Christians, we are the church, so how can each one of us give support to those who are helpless?

Jesus supports us, so we must pass that blessing on to others. John said, "Whoever says, 'I abide in him,' ought to walk just as he walked" (1 John 2:6).

First, we can be strong Christians. The writer of Hebrews said, "Lift your drooping hands and strengthen your weak knees" (Heb 12:12).

Isaiah said, "Strengthen the weak hands, and make firm the feeble knees. Say to those who are of a fearful heart, 'Be strong, do not fear!'" (Isa 35:3–4).

Then we can be aware of needs around us. Jesus described the kinds of support needed: "Then the king will say to those at his right hand, 'Come, you that are blessed by my Father, inherit the kingdom prepared for you from the foundation of the world; for I was hungry and you gave me food, I was thirsty and you gave me something to drink, I was a stranger and you welcomed me, I was naked and you gave me clothing, I was sick and you took care of me, I was in prison and you visited me'" (Matt 25:34–36). Then he explained that when we serve others, we are serving him.

Paul said, "I have given you an example that by such work we must support the weak, remembering the words of the Lord Jesus, for he himself said, 'It is more blessed to give than to receive'" (Acts 20:35).

Later he said, "We who are strong ought to put up with the failings of the weak" (Rom 15:1).

We can have a compassionate spirit. We can share our resources. We can teach and counsel.

In the story about the branches and the vine, Jesus illustrated the need for spiritual connections. As he strengthens us, we must strengthen others.

Weak Christians are unproductive. When someone suffers a stroke, it often leaves them paralyzed on one side. Even though they have lost the function of an arm or a leg, they may still have to carry it around. Some church members are like that. They're just dead weights. Fortunately, with a lot of determined discipline and therapy, these useless limbs can be restored. That's what happens when a weak individual receives support and strength.

Without support the results of weakness can be tragic. Debilitating or terminal illness, death of a loved one, loss of ability to support their family, and other uncontrollable circumstances can leave people feeling completely helpless. Helplessness is a terrifying thing. We resist it. We deny it. Then when we finally come face to face with it, we may be unable to endure it.

Everyone needs support at some point in their life. Even Jesus needed it in the garden of Gethsemane when his disciples slept. In fact, Jesus promised us his own spiritual presence. But sometimes we also need a more concrete and physical presence. The church can be such a support group. Members of a church congregation can uphold and comfort and strengthen each other in times of stress and grief.

We can take three lessons from this message: First, realize that helplessness is destructive. Everybody needs support and strength. Next, understand that the Christian church is the chief organization here on this earth to fulfill that need. Therefore, let's make our church more supportive and helpful. Finally, believe that personal support is a gift from God to you. When you incorporate that constant feeling of support into your own life, then you will find ways to extend it to others, and this will eventually change the world. And that's the purpose of the church of the twenty-first century.

[1]Annie J. Flint, *He Giveth More Grace*, (Hayden Press: 2019) 3.

Purpose

Edward Hale in 1902 said, "I am only one, but still I am one. I cannot do everything, but still I can do something. And because I cannot do everything, I will not refuse to do the something that I can do."[1]

Will Rogers, American entertainer, is often quoted as saying, "If you want to be successful, it's just this simple. Know what you're doing, love what you're doing, and believe in what you're doing."

People in our world today need purpose.

Have you ever felt aimless? Maybe you didn't know what friends to choose. Maybe you didn't know which classes to take in college. Maybe you didn't know which occupation to prepare for. Maybe you didn't know which interests to pursue. Maybe you didn't know which investments to make. Maybe you didn't know which charities to support.

Aimlessness hurts. People who don't have a purpose waste precious time and energy on dead-end jobs. Jesus knew that purpose is a deep, universal need. That's why he gave every Christian a specific assignment: "You will be my witnesses" (Acts 1:8).

Jesus not only stated the purpose of our lives in words; he demonstrated it. He spent his time on earth being a witness. He exemplified the character of God, saying, "Whoever has seen me has seen the Father" (John 14:9).

He served, even at age twelve, saying, "I must be in my Father's house!" (Luke 2:49).

He fulfilled his purpose on the cross, saying, "I glorified you on earth by finishing the work that you gave me to do" (John 17:4).

Jesus also told a story about the importance of purpose and productivity:

> A nobleman went to a distant country to get royal power for himself and then return. He summoned ten of his slaves, and gave them ten pounds, and said to them, "Do business with these until I come back." But the citizens of his country hated him and sent a delegation after him, saying, "We do not want this man to rule over us." When he returned, having received royal power, he ordered these slaves, to whom he had given the money, to be summoned so that he might find out what they had gained by trading. The first came forward and said,

"Lord, your pound has made ten more pounds." He said to him, "Well done, good slave! Because you have been trustworthy in a very small thing, take charge of ten cities." Then the second came, saying, "Lord, your pound has made five pounds." He said to him, "And you, rule over five cities." Then the other came, saying, "Lord, here is your pound. I wrapped it up in a piece of cloth, for I was afraid of you, because you are a harsh man; you take what you did not deposit, and reap what you did not sow." He said to him, "I will judge you by your own words, you wicked slave! You knew, did you, that I was a harsh man, taking what I did not deposit and reaping what I did not sow? Why then did you not put my money into the bank? Then when I returned, I could have collected it with interest." He said to the bystanders, "Take the pound from him and give it to the one who has ten pounds. (And they said to him, "Lord, he has ten pounds!") I tell you, to all those who have, more will be given; but from those who have nothing, even what they have will be taken away." (Luke 19:11–26)

This story clearly shows that we are to find our niche, discover our purpose, and use wisely the gifts and abilities God has given us.

The church of the twenty-first century must fill this need for purpose.

Every organization, program, and service of the Lord's church must emphasize purpose. Unfortunately, that hasn't always been the case. Too often, religions, denominations, and churches have floundered. They offer hit-or-miss activities. They preach sermons that are trite or impractical. They do no long-term planning to ensure that their teachings cover all the topics and issues people so desperately need. As a result, members of the congregation get shallow information. The writer of Hebrews describes such a situation: "By this time you ought to be teachers, you need someone to teach you again the basic elements of the oracles of God. You need milk, not solid food; for everyone who lives on milk, being still an infant, is unskilled in the word of righteousness. But solid food is for the mature" (Heb 5:12–14).

A church that has a purpose encourages its members to fulfill their mission. This requires good foresight and organization. It requires information about the different temperaments and talents and skills of its members. Such churches must do research to discover the needs of the people in its area. Fitting different members to the various jobs and offices is crucial. For example, a person who would make a wonderful youth director would probably be a total failure as a treasurer or bookkeeper and vice versa. One who is a wonderful soloist or pianist may not know how to work with children. A great carpenter or mechanic may not be a good teacher. Each of us has our own special gifts for service, and these must be developed and utilized. Peter said, "Serve one another with whatever gift each of you has received" (1 Peter 4:10).

In short, a church that emphasizes purpose analyzes its community and its congregation. It matches gifts to needs, realizing that anytime you see a need you can fill, that should be seen as a call from God.

One of the twelve apostles, Andrew, showed evangelistic tendencies from the beginning. The scriptures say, "He first found his brother Simon and said to him, 'We have found the Messiah' (which is translated Anointed). He brought Simon to Jesus" (John 1:41–42).

Jesus called him from his occupation as a fisherman and gave him a specific mission: "He saw Simon and his brother Andrew casting a net into the sea—for they were fishermen. And Jesus said to them, 'Follow me and I will make you fish for people.' And immediately they left their nets and followed him" (Mark 1:16–18)

Andrew was also the one who brought the child with the loaves and fishes to Jesus (see John 6:8–9). Later, he brought a group of Greeks to Jesus (see John 12:20–22).

What would have happened if, when Jesus called, Andrew had answered, "No way, Lord. I love to fish. Following you is just too hard"? Peter and many others may not have found the Lord. That's why the church of the twenty-first century must emphasize purpose in life.

Remember, in the story Jesus told, those who utilized the talents they were given were rewarded for having initiative and for being productive. The one who didn't use his talents was severely punished and lost his talents.

When Jesus gives us a calling and a purpose, he expects us to follow and fulfill the mission. That's what Andrew did. We must do likewise!

Now, Let's Get Personal.

As individual Christians, we are the church, so how can each one of us help those who are aimless to discover their purpose in life?

Jesus gave us a purpose, so we must pass that characteristic on to others. John said, "Whoever says, 'I abide in him,' ought to walk just as he walked" (1 John 2:6).

First, we must exemplify purpose. Our lives must be focused on the "best" things. We must be productive and efficient. A life based on a moral and spiritual foundation accomplishes positive and constructive results.

We must not be apathetic and wasteful like the man with the one talent. Many scriptures admonish us to be industrious in the use of our resources. Solomon even urges us to learn from insects. He said, "Go to the ant, you lazybones; consider its ways, and be wise" (Prov 6:6).

He also emphasized a good work ethic, saying, "Do you see those who are skillful in their work? They will serve kings" (Prov 22:29).

The writer of Ecclesiastes wrote, "Whatever your hand finds to do, do with your might" (Eccl 9:10).

Paul said, "Do not lag in zeal, be ardent in spirit, serve the Lord" (Rom 12:11).

He even practiced "tough love" when he said, "Even when we were with you, we gave you this command: Anyone unwilling to work should not eat" (2 Thess 3:10).

Too often, religion has majored on negatives, telling adherents what not to do. One man told of meeting a fellow on the street who was most eager to tell him about his church. He said, "Our church is more spiritual than yours because we make everyone sign this covenant that says, 'I will not gamble. I will not play cards. I will not smoke. I will not tell off-color jokes." And so on and so on.

The first man pointed to his dog sleeping nearby. "You know, mister, my old hound dog don't do none of them things either. I guess I must have a very spiritual dog."

This approach is narrow and arrogant. Christianity is different. It majors on positives. Jesus was more interested in what individuals did do than in what they didn't do.

The unhappiest people in the world are those who have not found something they want to do. You can find your purpose in life by analyzing your abilities, praying, studying Scripture, listening to advice, taking advantage of opportunities, and fulfilling your heart's desires.

In the story about the servants and their investments, Jesus illustrated the importance of being active and productive.

A man training a rescue dog watched him stop to sniff a rabbit and then become distracted by a ball. The trainer said, "His faculties may be excellent, but his focus is lacking. Until he learns to prioritize and stay on task, he's useless as a rescue dog."

It's the same with us. We must prioritize and focus and stay on task if we're to fulfill our purpose. God is extremely concerned about us reaching our potential. How foolish it would have been for Beethoven to have dreamed of becoming a politician. He would have committed a serious "sin of omission" if he had not made a contribution to the world through his music. What wasted effort it would have been if Einstein had dreamed of being a movie star and neglected to make a contribution to the world through his science. God has a purpose for each of us.

We can take three lessons from this message: First, realize that purposelessness is destructive. Everybody needs a purpose. Next, understand that the Christian church is the chief organization here on this earth to fulfill that need. Therefore, let's emphasize purpose in all of our organizations and programs and encourage our members to develop their own special talents and abilities. Finally, believe that purpose is a gift from God to you. When you incorporate that feeling of purpose into your own life, then you will find ways to enable others to use their gifts, and this will eventually change the world. And that's the purpose of the church of the twenty-first century.

[1]*A Year of Beautiful Thoughts* (1902) by Jeanie Ashley Bates Greenough, p. 172.

Hope

People in the world today need hope.

Have you ever felt hopeless? Maybe your plans failed. Maybe there seems to be no light at the end of the tunnel. Maybe you are grieving a loss. Maybe you are depressed and despondent. Maybe problems are overwhelming you. Maybe you see all the evil and crime in the world and just give up. Depression is so prevalent that it's called the common cold of mental illness. Unfortunately, this emotional state takes away our productivity and our happiness.

Hopelessness hurts! Sometimes people who lose heart become unproductive and apathetic. They may even resort to destructive acts such as homicide or suicide.

Christians have many promises concerning hope. Paul said, "May the God of hope fill you with all joy and peace in believing, so that you may abound in hope by the power of the Holy Spirit" (Rom 15:13).

The writer of Hebrews said, "We have this hope, a sure and steadfast anchor of the soul" (Heb 6:19)

Jesus knew that hope is a deep, universal need. He said, "In the world you face persecution. But take courage; I have conquered the world!" (John 16:33).

Jesus not only talked about hope in words; he demonstrated it. Over and over, he portrayed positive attitudes and joy. He constantly reminded his followers of his own joy in life. He says, "I speak these things in the world so that they may have my joy made complete in themselves" (John 17:13).

Jesus was optimistic, saying, "Rejoice that your names are written in heaven" (Luke 10:20).

Jesus also told a story about hope and optimism:

> The kingdom of heaven may be compared to someone who sowed good seed in his field; but while everybody was asleep, an enemy came and sowed weeds among the wheat, and then went away. So when the plants came up and bore grain, then the weeds appeared as well. And the slaves of the householder came and said to him, "Master, did you not sow good seed in your field? Where, then, did these weeds come from?" He answered, "An enemy has done this." The slaves said to him, "Then do you want us to go and gather them?" But he replied,

"No; for in gathering the weeds you would uproot the wheat along with them. Let both of them grow together until the harvest; and at harvest time I will tell the reapers, Collect the weeds first and bind them in bundles to be burned, but gather the wheat into my barn." (Matt 13:24–30)

This story clearly shows that there is always hope, even when things look hopeless. We don't have to spend all our time trying to eradicate sins. We don't have to worry about evil triumphing. We are assured that good will win.

The church of the twenty-first century must fill this need for hope.

Every organization, program, and service of the Lord's church must give hope. Unfortunately, that hasn't always been the case. Too often, religions, denominations, and churches have emphasized hellfire and damnation over love and joy. They have blamed and threatened instead of reassuring and promising victory. As a result, needy, depressed, and hopeless individuals have avoided the church and gone to bars and cocktail parties that give them at least a brief respite from gloom and misery.

Jesus never sat around wringing his hands and moaning about the world going to hell in a handbasket. He said, "I have said these things to you so that my joy may be in you, and that your joy may be complete" (John 15:11).

A hopeful church is positive and optimistic. It doesn't dwell on what is wrong. It points out what's right. The message and lessons and activities are all forward-looking and joyful. The leaders do not use fear tactics and intimidation to influence the members. Such a church does not waste its time regretting the mistakes of the past. Instead, it maximizes the productive actions of the present and looks expectantly toward a hope-filled future.

Jesus gave hope to small churches when he said, "The kingdom of heaven is like a mustard seed that someone took and sowed in his field; it is the smallest of all the seeds, but when it has grown it is the greatest of shrubs and becomes a tree, so that the birds of the air come and make nests in its branches" (Matt 13:31–32).

Here we are promised that even the smallest grain of truth and righteousness will have unbelievable consequences over the long term. Small efforts are important. They leave ripples that reach out. Jesus said, "Whoever gives even a cup of cold water to one of these little ones in the name of a disciple—truly I tell you, none of these will lose their reward" (Matt 10:42).

He also reassured us that large numbers and great promotions are not necessarily evidence of success: "Where two or three are gathered in my name, I am there among them" (Matt 18:20).

In short, a church of hope will allow its members to leave services feeling better about themselves and better prepared for another week in a fallen world.

The thief on the cross had gone his last mile—no more opportunities, no more time, not even twenty-four hours. That day truly was his only "day of salvation." The scriptures say,

> Two others also, who were criminals, were led away to be put to death with him…. One of the criminals who were hanged there kept deriding him and saying, "Are you not the Messiah? Save yourself and us!" But the other rebuked him, saying, "Do you not fear God, since you are under the same sentence of condemnation? And we indeed have been condemned justly, for we are getting what we deserve for our deeds, but this man has done nothing wrong." Then he said, "Jesus, remember me when you come into your kingdom." He replied, "Truly I tell you, today you will be with me in Paradise." (Luke 23:32, 39–43)

That's why the church of the twenty-first century must offer hope.

Remember, in the story Jesus told, the workers didn't need to despair over all the evils they saw because they were assured that the good seed would win. There is always hope even for an unworthy thief in his dying hour.

Now, Let's Get Personal.

As individual Christians, we are the church, so how can each one of us give hope to those who are hopeless?

Jesus gave us hope, so we must pass that blessing on to others. John said, "Whoever says, 'I abide in him,' ought to walk just as he walked" (1 John 2:6).

First, our lives must reflect our hope. No one wants to be around negative people who constantly point out the flaws of others and the evils of the world. We must never start or spread gossip and rumors. And when they come to us, we must stop them. However, if we hear compliments or positive statements, these should always be repeated and passed on. We must also read and share scriptures that lift up.

The psalmist said, "Be strong, and let your heart take courage, all you who wait for the LORD" (Ps 31:24).

The psalmist also said, "I will hope continually" (Ps 71:14).

Solomon said, "The hope of the righteous ends in gladness, but the expectation of the wicked comes to nothing" (Prov 10:28).

He also said, "Hope deferred makes the heart sick" (Prov 13:12).

Without the gift of hope, the world would be a different place. Columbus looking to the western horizon would have told his crew, "There doesn't seem to be anything in sight. Let's turn around and go home."

George Washington, surveying his ragged forces at Valley Forge, would have surrendered.

Thomas Alva Edison, after spending forty thousand dollars to test filaments for an electric light, would have shrugged and said, "I give up. Nobody will ever figure this out."

Losing hope leads to despair. Years ago, Florence Chadwick fell short in her effort to swim across the English Channel. She said in a news conference the next day that the fog was too heavy, and she could not see the shore. Had she been able to see it, she believed she would have made it across. That's the Christian view of life. It sees the shore. It sees God as both the alpha and omega of human existence.

Hope is powerful. Survivors of Nazi concentration camps were often not necessarily the most physically fit. Instead, they usually had a loved one waiting or had some great goal to realize. Hope is life preserving.

A group of children were watching the movie Snow White. When the witch appeared, the children were terrified. At the height of the confusion, a little girl stood up on her seat and called for attention. "Please listen!" she yelled. "My mommy has read me this story many times, and it comes out all right in the end." That's the Christian hope!

We can take three lessons from this message: First, realize that lack of hope is deadly. Everybody needs to feel hope. Next, understand that the Christian church is the chief organization here on this earth to fulfill that need. Therefore, let's work to keep our church hopeful. Finally, believe that hope is a gift from God to you. When you incorporate that feeling of hope into your own life, then you will find ways to extend it to others, and this will eventually change the world. And that's the purpose of the church of the twenty-first century.

Conclusion

As Christians we're not called to be religious. As Christians we're not called to be pious. As Christians we're not called to be sanctimonious. Instead, we're called to enjoy a real, free and productive life. Jesus said, "I am come that they might have life, and that they might have it more abundantly" (John 10:10, KJV).

Too often the gospel is presented in a negative way. People are led to believe that God wants everyone to be sad and somber with no zest for life. Some theological creeds and quite a lot of medieval art depicts Christianity like that, but the gospel doesn't. Jesus was a vital, interesting, and magnetic person. Children loved him. He attracted fishermen and government officials, beggars and kings, scholars and tradesmen. In short, he was a regular guy.

It's unfortunate that we always seem to picture him with a halo and white robe, instead of jeans and boots. Actually, Jesus was so normal looking and acting that Judas had to point him out in the crowd. He went to parties. He built houses. He had friends. He lived a full life and he offers such a life to us. So, what is abundant life?

First, a person with abundant life is real. Jesus was speaking to religious leaders when he said, "You are those who justify yourselves in the sight of others; but God knows your hearts; for what is prized by human beings is an abomination in the sight of God" (Luke 16:15).

 He also said, "This people honors me with their lips, but their hearts are far from me" (Matt 15:8).

Paul said, "They profess to know God, but they deny him by their actions. They are detestable, disobedient, unfit for any good work" (Titus 1:16).

John said, "Whoever says, 'I have come to know him,' but does not obey his commandments, is a liar, and in such a person the truth does not exist" (1 John 2:4).

God doesn't approve of hypocrisy. God wants us to be honest and authentic. Becoming a Christian does not require us to change our basic temperament. Instead, God wants us to discover and reveal our own special personality. God wants us to be who we were meant to be.

There is no one way to be a Christian. Paul was nothing like Peter. Barnabas was very different from James and John. It's okay that some Christians are lively and sociable. It's okay that some Christians are organized and work oriented. It's okay that some Christians are quiet and reflective. It's okay that some Christians are laid back and easy going. God loves and accepts all kinds of people.

Paul said, "We have gifts that differ according to the grace given to us: prophecy, in proportion to faith; ministry, in ministering; the teacher, in teaching; the exhorter, in exhortation; the giver, in generosity; the leader, in diligence; the compassionate, in cheerfulness" (Rom 12:6-8).

We are also called to follow our own particular interests. Everyone has certain desires and passions. These are given to us for a reason. Nature lovers, bookworms, sports enthusiasts, and antique collectors are all accepted and encouraged in God's kingdom. Differences make life rich and fulfilling. Paul said, "For as in one body we have many members, and not all the members have the same function, so we, who are many, are one body in Christ, and individually we are members one of another" (Rom. 12:4-5).

"Now there are varieties of gifts, but the same Spirit" (1 Cor. 12:4).

Most importantly, we are each called to use our own unique talents and skills. God gives every person certain aptitudes and abilities. It takes all of these to meet the needs of humanity. God doesn't want us to waste any of the gifts given to us. Paul said, "Do not neglect the gift that is in you . . ." (1 Tim 4:14).

Peter said, "Serve one another with whatever gift each of you has received" (1 Pet 4:10).

So, to live an abundant life we must be real.

Next, a person with abundant life is free. Jesus said, "You will know the truth, and the truth will make you free" (John 8:32).

We're called to be free of guilt. Wallowing in remorse, obsessing about past mistakes, regretting poor decisions and living with shame about improper actions are a waste of time. The Psalmist said, "Happy are those whose transgression is forgiven, whose sin is covered. Happy are those to whom the Lord imputes no iniquity, and in whose spirit there is no deceit" (Ps 32:1-2).

Isaiah said, "I have swept away your transgressions like a cloud, and your sins like mist; return to me, for I have redeemed you" (Isa 44:22).

The writer of Hebrews said, "I will remember their sins and their lawless deeds no more" (Heb 10:17).

If God forgets our evil acts, why can't we?

We are also called to be free of fear. Living with fear and anxiety and dread leads to tension and depression. It nullifies our joy, undermines our productivity and sabotages our success. Isaiah said, "Surely God is my salvation; I will trust, and will not be afraid . . ." (Isa 12:2).

Jesus said, "Peace I leave with you; my peace I give to you. I do not give to you as the world gives. Do not let your hearts be troubled, and do not let them be afraid" (John 14:27).

Paul said, "God did not give us a spirit of cowardice, but rather a spirit of power and of love and of self-discipline" (2 Tim 1:7).

We are definitely called to be free of bitterness. Holding on to hatred and hostility will destroy both our physical and emotional health. Nursing grudges saps our energy. Plotting revenge is detrimental. Like an acid, animosity eats away the vessel it's stored in. Solomon said, "Those who despise their neighbors are sinners . . ." (Prov 14:21).

Paul said, "Put away from you all bitterness and wrath and anger and wrangling and slander, together with all malice" (Eph 4:31).

Jesus himself said, "Love your enemies and pray for those who persecute you" (Matt 5:44).

So, to live an abundant life we must be free.

Finally, a person with abundant life is productive. Jesus said, "We must work the works of him who sent me while it is day . . ." (John 9:4).

Later he described it this way: "The harvest is plentiful, but the laborers are few; therefore ask the Lord of the harvest to send out laborers into his harvest" (Luke 10:2).

For Christians, service to others is essential. Busy people are happy and successful people.

Our first responsibility is to make our family better. Kindness, like charity, should start at home. Our own loved ones deserve our time and our resources. Being concerned for the welfare of our husbands and wives, for our mothers and fathers, and for our children is a basic requirement. Providing for necessities, listening to opinions, solving problems, and ensuring that there's a pleasant atmosphere in our home as we share meals and chores is important. Solomon said, "Enjoy life with the wife whom you love . . ." (Eccl 9:9).

Paul said, "The husband should give to his wife her conjugal rights, and likewise the wife to her husband" (1 Cor 7:3).

He also said, "Fathers, do not provoke your children to anger, but bring them up in the discipline and instruction of the Lord" (Eph 6:4).

He even said, "Whoever does not provide for relatives, and especially for family members, has denied the faith and is worse than an unbeliever" (1 Tim 5:8).

We're also called to make our community better. This includes developing good relationships with neighbors and avoiding gossip about associates. It means increasing the safety of our streets and adding to the beauty of our parks. It means supporting charitable institutions. Solomon said, "Do not withhold good from those to whom it is due, when it is in your power to do it" (Prov 3:27).

Paul said, "Each of us must please our neighbor for the good purpose of building up the neighbor" (Rom 15:2).

"So then, whenever we have an opportunity, let us work for the good of all, and especially for those of the family of faith" (Gal 6:10).

He said we are to be role models. "Set the believers an example in speech and conduct, in love, in faith, in purity" (1 Tim 4:12).

In fact, as Christians, we are called to make our world a better place. Jesus said, "You will receive power when the Holy Spirit has come upon you; and you will be my witnesses in Jerusalem, in all Judea and Samaria, and to the ends of the earth" (Acts 1:8).

When we are told to witness, to share our faith and to bring in the Kingdom, that means we are to spend our time doing things that will make life on this earth more enjoyable. It means we're to preserve and care for all of God's creation. It means we're to value each other and the resources God has provided.

Our relationships, our careers, our recreation and our hobbies should all include actions that will promote beauty, joy, peace, and love. Solomon said, "Whatever your hand finds to do, do with your might . . ." (Eccl 9:10).

Paul said, "So we are ambassadors for Christ, since God is making his appeal through us . . ." (2 Cor 5:20). So, to live an abundant life, we must be productive.

As Christians, we're called to be real. We are to use our special personalities, our skills, our experiences, our interests, and our talents to the fullest. We're to be free of guilt, fear, and bitterness by accepting God's forgiveness and then forgiving ourselves. We're to be productive in our family, in our community and in the world. This is the abundant life God promised when he said, "I know what I have planned for you . . . I have good plans for you. I don't plan to hurt you. I plan to give you hope and a good future" (see Jer 29:11).

This is what Jesus meant when he said, "I am come that they might have life, and that they might have it . . . abundantly" (John 10:10, KJV).

CPSIA information can be obtained
at www.ICGtesting.com
Printed in the USA
BVHW041406221121
622236BV00013B/412

9 781635 281514